SHORT
WORKS

SHORT WORKS
POEMS AND
OTHER WRITINGS

ROSS TOMKINS

McHoo

email: authors@mc-hoo.com

ISBN: 978 0 9553696 1 2

First published in 2014 by McHoo

for Sophia Perennis

Contents

Poems

Poems from Poems

Stories

Poems
1965 – 2014

Elephants' Graveyard

In deep wax-green forests shady
With chirk chirr bright trogons flutter
And flash red-gold pennoncel feathers
Amongst murmur branches stirring.
Leopard curl tight-soft to trunk of
Pollen-dusty buttress rooted.
Flex your claws, sigh, hear growl.
The trogon chirrs, branch jumps, flies
Into gloomy reaches of dark leaf-mould.
Sniffle porcupine nosing soft,
Gnaw the yellowed ivory: dust.
Nudge the rib, lying pallid
Deep in dry crushed leaf and twig.
Sniff through empty orbits,
Sleep with the ants
In the pitted tusks, end-splintered.
Tiny world, where spider reigns
Beneath a leaf.
Toad winks, blinks and gulps
Wings sticking tattered to damp lips.
Moth catches sunlight on her pale
Mica wing-fur.
And her antenna twitch softly.
Dithers nervously into air, white speck.

Death by Water

flumina te angunt florentibus undique ripis

Among swaying rushes,
Lapped by soft ripples,
Where the bittern roll-booms,
Where the moorhen dabbles,
Among the slender osiers,
Face-down murky lapping

The wind whistles moaning,
Twining tight the flashing reeds,
Caressing the blue-grey skin
Puffed by water's rub
The pale lamphrey coils sliding
About a leg, tattered
Rags wafting apart by ebb,
By flow, weft and warp,
And so, sinew, hair,
Skin, tendon and thew.

Chubb chumbles mouthing white
Flesh beneath the moon.
A far white horse gallops
Splash up spray as liquid
Silver tinkle quiet.
Birds shiver in whistling air.
Winter to spring, summer,
And turn, and turn, till only
White, cleaned, water-supple
Bones remain. Mere glimpse of
A shin shining in the
Decaying sedge of this mud islet.
Refuge from pike and eel for
Thin red-legged moorhen.
Autumn's debris,
Gleam gone.

Dog-days

The yellow skull of a dog,
Odour from some dank cavern,
Lies brindled amongst dog-bramble.
Ghosts baying the damp moon
Echo in the broken brick and dust.
Dog groan in the deep nettleweed;
Dog whines curl up in rusty cans.
I remember hide and seek
And a dog dead under a bush,
Its pebble-teeth scattering the path,
Its clammy skull staring
And mouthing taboo.

Frozen Land

Ice drops drift the frozen air,
Bluecold prisms flashing death.
Pine boughs, stippled with frost ribs,
Wearily dip to skim the snow.
Rabbit, winterthin, bounds
Fearful — fawn dapple white;
Brown eyes swell, ears streamline,
Steamy breath melts the glistening mist.
Hawk hangs in glazed coldhaze, pitched high,
Curls on the wingbeat, blue eye probes clear.
Wind slices through screaming pinions,
Red pincers hammer-snatch.
Away, high and away, to clanging peaks,
Steel-clouded ice-shattered blocks
Piled on the dead earth.
High raw-slashing windflows.
Marrowfreezing water seeps to the pale sun,
Snowcrust crackles, fades thin.
Green slivers pierce the snow.

Noctule

Midnight. Mad nocturne dreaming as
The brain drowsily draws breath,
Aching out another heavy-lid hour.
My adolescent pen doodles morbidities
As the moonclock ticks in her tower.
Footsteps on the stair,
Mutterings in corners, until finally
Leather-rustly bats sail the room,
And I row the dank night on their wings,
To rank churchyards and mudflat reaches
Where the chained felon swings
Above a sullen tide.

Mad Suibne

Cold winds, spinning off the fluff white sun,
Whistle fast across moorland and estuary,
Chase each other in screaming whorls
Around ivy'd boles of stunted trees,
Flinging whipping cold into the averted face
Of a man, no man.

Once a real face, ruddy and round —
Now it pinches, drawing flesh from the skull,
Squeezing a nose, scaly with grey frost.

Suibne jams his frame into the tree in the wind;
His body weighs nothing;
Shadow in birdlike form.

Suibne jumps the air, blinks
Again at the madman's wisp.
Suibne struck the priest,
Who flung the straw,
Which confused eye and brain.
Suibne fled, stumbling in his blindness,
Driven from men, lodging in trees,
Eating grass, milking uneasy cattle
At night. Not bird, nor man, nor wind.
Mad Suibne!

River Lizard

Blunt peaks break water,
The black mace of the crocodile.
Sardonic blood runs in her veins.

Leviathan

Sea winds whip splintered spars
Snatching woodpulp into the howling flood
Molten glass, pearlspray spattering.
Water chains thrash the ship, back broken.
The ghostly rock-teeth gullet yawns wide.
The ship drawn like a dazzled moth
To the swinging red coal of the wreckers' lamp,
Hanging in the maw-black screaming skies.
Dead whale stranded on the silent foreshore —
Ripped rags of seagulls squabble on the flesh.

Willow Month

Willow month
Time of the running waters
The drowned man
And a lean hawk
Dipping in a gravel stream
And a pale toadstool
Fleshy and sicksweet
Bursting the maidenhead
Of rotting wet fern.
A spider drowning
In his globy web.
Time of the child
Born from the sea
And men standing
Singing on the shore
The booming surf
Drums beneath the sky
As stunted creatures
Rise and fall
The flash along the blade
Dividing cold from cold

Tom Cox's Traverse

The mad king squats upon his throne
Propped amongst the weeds
Broken pillars form his court
Each stump topped by an attendant toad
Rain courses the harlequin floors
Cross-hatched by tufted grass
And outside this ruined palace
Desolation

Skeletal cows with burst udders sprawl
On shattered brown brittlegrass
Here the parch sun swings high
Never cooled by swathing clouds
Fish gasp in the cracked river mud
Fire and smoke jump tree to tree
Orange the land chokes with the dust
Of its desolation

There is a stillness in the air
Sightless skulls stare into space
Trees sway leafless silently
Shrivelled deer watch from the forest shade
Every creeping thing upon the earth
Peers at the broken palace
For a mad king to finish with
This desolation

Fat black corbies jeeringly sport
In hypnotic circles about the ruined turrets
The cemetery under the rose garden
Yawns to push forth its phosphorescent dead.
Brittle spiders spin again
In murmuring garrets
To snare rejuvenated flies
All feed all spawn on
This desolation

→

But there must be some life some vigour
Beneath this cracked soil
Somewhere the white figures wait
To stroll again in the rose garden.
Where is the stranger to purge
Away the disease festering here
To cauterize the roots of
This desolation

Roses thrive on old corruptions
Clouds have piled up on this land's drought
Some seed will sprout
The rainbringing stranger sits
Even now on the abused throne
And will stir again to health
And make an end to this desolation.

Dragon Womb

The worm turns its long screw
Beneath the grass
An owl blinks bitterly
In a deep wood of mauve
Where I wander lost
Drawn in respiralled spirals
Slowly to the navel of this wood
My uncertain path crossed
By stag and red-eared hounds

Sometimes I follow paths lit from high
Or push through black thickets
With snaking iron-spiked branches
Or, sleepwalk through haze,
Face-whipping saplings
— But always travelling towards the colder.

Trees grow rimy — breath clouds my view.
A tinkling landscape snaps beneath my feet
Skin-tingling ice invades my clothes
Chill, perplexed, wondering
     Dead birds light as tumbled weed
Maybe I've been here some time
     Litter the hoarfrosted grass spikes
Before ... I don't know
It's so cold. My bones feel brittle
No flesh on them
So cold

The Singing Sands

Poison-spangled serpents drift from their rocks
Under an opal moon
Metallic scorpions scuttle
On unthinking insect forays
And red-eyed timorous jerboas
Shuddering, jump for the next spurt of grass
Cold winds sweep across the sand
Dimpled by the jackal's loping slot.
Lost land of Cambyses' legions,
Of cold-eyed Senussi tribes.
One drop of dew hangs beneath each stone
Distilled from the yellow hornèd moon,
Refracting the ice of a million stars

S a l i n a s

Below the granite-stacked mesas
And their rubble-covered feet
At the low of ever-thirsting sand basins
Lie the dead silver salt-pans,
Encrusting skeletons with their brittle snow
Which sucks all moisture from the bone
Distilling this solid dew
Which will relieve no thirst

Parisian Interlude

Experience drops from the net
Into the killing jar, chokes
On crushed laurel,
Is catalogued, set, pinned
And mounted in an
Entomologist's back room.

On the banks of the Seine
We watched the sodden debris
Drift downstream, orange peel,
Inscrutable oily globules,
All severally catching the eye,
Drawing it on down with them.
We reclined in dust and dry dung
To watch the flow of the city's garbage
Between the barges and the quais;
Thus we knew the city better than any tourist
Watching the intestinal river drag home to the sea.

We slept by the river and
Caught the Nice express
On a one-way ticket
Early in the morning.

Nauagon

Dead too is Aias
Long oars of his galley
Split and shred like bamboo

The running storm waves
Fling the ship like a javelin
Onto the rocks
Of Gyrae

Remember those who walked in an arid valley
Dry under the mortmain of the fixed black stars
Of dust are their spirit

Aias' spirit runs with the waves
Dilutes itself into the watery element
This is his reincarnation

Antipodal Spring

The deep and marbled halls of sleep
Mute footman's eyes show no great surprise
A country summer and to the queen's court
I return with tales of foreign itineraries
Dark her eyes in the darkness
I slept in my awakening
Now I awake in my slumbering
My dreams lack no reality
My buds burst as the leaves turn

The Band on the Mail Train

The band plays the electric darkness
Controlled rhythmic drum thunder
Guitar licks fast as thought
Flicker like phosphorescent jack in the box lizards
Guitars flash back the arc lights
Slow explosions of bass runs
The song strains to a mathematical guitar counterpoint
Like a black locomotive
Iron horse galloping the mails
The band roars into the night
All lights steam and noise

Werewolf

Sickle moon and the wolves running
Icy air webs the black pylon trees
Mental wilderness of black and white
And the quicksilver wolves running
Yellow moon in the indigo sky
A man walks this forest, the snow
Explodes quietly under his feet, fog breath.
Wolves taste the man scent
Soft whump of snowfall from branches
Amber eyes cluster the subarboreal gloom
Dropping to all fours he rejoins his pack

Palingenesis

Tiger growls deep in my soul
Tiger prowls deep dank rain forest
Monkeys hoot in the night-time trees
Tiger shoulders the scraping elephant grass
Rock men above the forest
Hear the cough nosing below
Feel the pads of each claw-heavy paw
Softly impress the ground, stripes surging
To the muscle heave.
Fires listen in the rock hills.
No wind dilutes the silence, no bird call
Breaks it

Historia Ventorum

Deep in a dry white arctic wilderness
Three crones in an unconscious cave
Whistle up a hyperboreal wind
Quintessence of white Pegasus
Pounds through tundra and steppe to blow
Open the crashing gates of this city
Windows rattle and dogs slink the streets
Peppered by the stinging dust clouds
The philosopher dozing in his tower chamber
Hears the wind shriek battering his shutters
The sudden stuffy oppression of his room
As horses gallop up-spiralling the tower
Raucous panic of rooks blown from their nest
Trees bend sensibly letting slip their dead

Orpheus at Alissa

And they took the head into a cave
Near where the juvenile stream joins the sea
And wiped away the clotted blood
Opened the pallid eyes and set it on a rock
In the interior darkness
Pungent with bat smell, dank with fungi
The eyes illuminated the lush gloom
And from the cave mouth pours an endless song
Whose rhythm is the breaking of the waves
Whose verses are the turning of the tides
So he sings as nature's proper tongue

Merlin

It was raining, Mars and Venus conjunct,
And in my island-hill's water-hollowed cave
I was carving in darkness
With cold chisel and mason's hammer
A bird of stone, gaunt with eyes of proud obsidian,
Each feather cut distinctly. Until it lay, wings
Outspread like my shadow on the stonedust.
A last tap, and I lifted it grunting,
Propped it against the wall, stood
Back and looked into its eyes. Close,
I breathed into its stony nostrils and respondent
Flames poured from its eyes. Stiffly the wings
Creak, muscles flex, talons scrape the floor.
Blindly he follows me to the cavemouth daylight,
Eyes glow with blue newborn fire drawn, perhaps by
chance,
To the sky-island clouds and their sun-rimmed beaches.
A beating roar of wings and there he flies, sun-gilded.
I watch apprehensively, shielding my eyes from the sun:
He does not look back.

The King Briefs His Spies

Come my familiar, squat upon my wrist,
Close your yellow eyes,
Whisper in my ear.
Approach you creatures of the dark,
Sit about my feet
Cluster of jade-green eyes.
Puss in Boots has come to report
The conversations of the giant
And has stolen me the golden egg.
Good, my cat, good, my familiar
Of the clock-tower eyes.
Go forth, hover in the lamplight,
Squat beside the hearth, creep along
The picture rail, listen in the cellar.
Be like spiders in the webs of your senses,
Fill your hands with whisperings,
Stuff your pockets with sidelong glances,
Burst your bags with rumour and confidences,
Come back and empty all at my feet.
Go Puss in Boots with your seven league strides,
Follow him you creatures, spread throughout the land.

Francisco and Rodriguez

...and Francisco and Rodriguez ?

Cutlass-slashed, and overboard,
Yonder the reef, there they loll
Together dead-drunk on a sandy bed
Silver coins stream from stove-in chests
Red silk wafts from their wounds.
And fuzzy-blue barracudas hang fingerwise
In that denser air about them.

A Fly Above The Mountains

A fly above the mountains
Blown by the floating winds
A mote secure in its helplessness
Riding an aerial storm

I would be
Dizzy above such chasms
Fearful of my suspension in nothingness
Offended by the driving winds
Sick for landfall

But to know oneself as just a fly in the sky
Is no small comfort;
With this knowledge comes a new:
Impotence is the same as power.

Fragments

Black candle to a black goddess
fire-bud floats like a lotus blossom
in the glass-black waxy pool
a dancing molten jewel

night that whispers
night of cat's fur
night of thick ink
ink that whispers
                Chaplin streetlamp tops up their heads
ink of cat's fur
                again with beer
night of thick ink
yellow idiot moon grins
three wade through ink
blind fingers grope
braille of the familiar streets leading home
ink-currents rush around them
cause them to stagger
sway
lurch

Vocative

Under your eyes
Gaunt rocks
Shiver and split
Pouring spring water
In abundance
Under your touch
Dry boughs
Tremble and quiver
Sprouting green buds
Hearing your voice
Cawing rooks
Fall silent
Unearthly fragrance
Drifts the woods
As you go by
A deep hush
Ripples through the forest surf
And birds fly above

You are the secret of the black masque
The knowledge of the darkness
The cleaver who is cleft
You are the desert traveller's dream
The unimaginable oasis
Lush and green
Hidden between the rolling dunes
Camelman's mirage of cool waters
Hovering in the glaring sky
Drunk at, yet always
Beyond the next horizon

$\longrightarrow$

You are the lost world
Over some high mountain pass
Within the blue mountains
Reached by a ragged band
No man who entered there
Lungs torn
Would seek another

Visas Are Unobtainable

"Visas are unobtainable and travellers may
encounter entry problems"

His cases labelled for a new and unknown destination
The traveller carefully rereads his timetables
Combs the uninformative guidebook
For some small reference to his journey's end
The book is punted beneath the bunk,
The timetables are jettisoned — for this destination
Cannot be plotted by when and where
There are borders to cross
But unmarked and innumerable
Its regions are the places we met
The bars we drank in, the car you drive
Its climate the way you were
Its capital unknown, its customs mysterious
And my liner blazing lights
Waits out at sea for landfall
And the exploration of the port
And possibly an end to the cruise

The Snake

Two o'clock and every light is out
The house breathes softly in its sleep
Your pet snake, still awake, glides
Over cool tiles onto the tickling
Geometry of the hall carpet,
And coils neatly under a chair.
Clack of the latch rouses it
Eyes of black glass unskin
As your front door opens, a blue shaft
Of light flecked with dust
Projects a blind stranger shuffle-
Sliding his feet, fingers fumbling
The walls, dabbing for the switch
Fast fangs slam his neck
Poison spurts down twinned rills;
Hand clasping the punctures
Slowly he falls backwards out
Through the closing door leaving
Another dead child on the floor.

Musings of Fantômas

No mass, no dimensions,
It cannot be seen,
The trail in the bubble chamber
Shows where it's been

And what is he looking for
When he cuts into the ground
Finding an empty chamber
In the centre of the mound?

Step into the labyrinth perhaps,
We imagine the smells
While the roars of the Minotaur
Smother the victim's yells

Unwrap the mummy then
Rip off its clothes
Defy its curses
Ignore its oaths

Could you imagine
If the mummy had eyes
What you might glimpse there
The staring surprise

Of collision with death
The very heaviest particle
Like an unfinished sentence
Stopping suddenly on the definite

Alone In My Bed ...

Alone in my bed, warm under quilt
And waiting for sleep
I hear the tiny pointed impacts —
One following dispersedly upon another —
Of raindrops on the panes.
I'd drawn, as usual, the curtains close
So no outer dark could penetrate,
Or warm air escape.
Is it rather tips of the fir-tree
Outside in the yard reaching over
And tapping, outside
Where a light night-wind blows?
Naturally, this morse was sent me plain
Clear the meaning behind my thought's words,
Clear who it might be, tapping at my window,
And had I jumped up and tugged on some clothes,
Scrambled downstairs then, three steps at a bound,
Stepped out onto the cold flags of the yard
Below my dark window to...
No sound, no-one, no-one just gone.
Summoned as I was to that glassy door
I should have run naked,
Burst through its frame —
But would anyone have been so daft?
It's only night and the night rain
Tapping at my window.
Later I hear the drone
Of a high plane passing slowly over
And I think of a sleigh
Skimming night's black snow

I Walked Right To The Back ...

I walked right to the back of the train
Stared hourlong through the little window
In the back of the last carriage of all.
Peering back down the long merging rails
To where those parallels fuse, knowing
That on that further impossible side
Beyond mere seeing
Station after station retreated
To that first unseeable terminus.
Useless from this low speeding vantage
To expect it all to stream directly
Into my bare unprotected eye.

Suddenly, then, I was flung on high,
Cushioned on air, and wind-chilled;
I could follow that track right back
To its origin, and even, riding the wind,
Be blown that way, and set down
Wheresoever I desired. But never forward.
No mere musclepower could beat through
That headwind, let me fly on ahead of the train,
Nor could I even so much as look forward,
As eyelids close against the wind's cold push.

$\rightarrow$

Though no hawk, from my tower,
I see all that gone-by landscape,
The park, the brick streets, and infants' school
Where held fast by a story read by our teacher
I sit in my own warm puddle
And between me and me
Not those thin twin steel lines
For timetabled trains and prearranged stations
But houses and gardens, cuttings and hedges,
Fields and squares, joined each to each
By roaring roads and hidden streams
Where birds fly down at will
To find their proper sustenance

From Your Own Correspondent

I should like to write to you,
Not a letter exactly — not to you —
Beginning, of course, with where I live
And the day on which I write,
And after the salutation I'd say
What I have to say to you,
Signing off with love, and my name.

I can't predict, though, on what day
You'll read it, nor in what place.
Your old addresses I can chase down
Back through all the months and years,
And through all those unexpected towns
Where you and I just happened to be living,
Sometimes just a few streets apart.

So I fold the page, envelope it,
Lean my blank-faced messenger
Against the mantelpiece wall,
Throw away the crossed-out streets
And the numbers that do not ring
But trusting that once more you're living
In some unknown near place to me,
To where all my letters can be sent
Once I've departed and moved on

Gas Fires Don't Hiss

Gas fires don't hiss, I thought,
But sigh, endlessly, hollowly,
Behind the fireclay gridwork
Where the burning, blue and mauve,
Washes rows of white-hot studs,
In imitation of a sunset

And the dusk sky outside
Burns with the same violet
Behind a fretwork of black trees
And a slanting row of yellow streetlights,
Each the centre of a softer fog,
Steps to an implied horizon,
In imitation of a gas fire.

And All The Trains Inside Me

And all the trains inside me
Keep running
Even when I'm not riding them

This driver in his black-curtained cab
Drops his battered leather satchel
Onto, is it, the dead man's wheel,
And eases the brakes.

The ticket collector with hunter's eyes
Haunts the aisles, and a darting
Bite of his small jaws kills
The pink ticket.

In the high signal box just past the station
The blur-faced man behind the grubby glass
Fists the thumbed levers and lights blink

Draught of cold, thuds, rock of the carriage
As solid phantoms alight or step aboard
At each squealing halt.
The dull seats wheeze dust like puffballs.

The eyes of strangers in unshared dreamtimes
Who ride this train unknowingly
While all the trains inside them
Clatter on
Even when they're not riding them

The White Sky

A white sky comes smashing down
Pale crabs skid out
Boxers half-blinded from their corners

Or, sodden logs are lifted
Snowflake insects
Acrid woodlice
Made of dustbins and buffalo horns
Scuttle to cover

Somewhere a toad gulps heavily
Jewel on a woman's breast

Twenty Fingers

In the deep dusk
Twenty dogs running lightly nose to shoulder
Flicker across the vlei and up between the hills
Soft-nosed they read the grass and thorns
My fingers brush over your body
And yours over mine

The Longboat

The longboat shudders into the beach
Its square stern drifts sideways
Salt-stiffened shirt and white pantaloons
A sailor plunges thighdeep into the surf
The boat's crew attend awkwardly; the officer
Nods. She rocks and swings and is empty

Jagged shadows clump the beach
The dark arm arcing down the seasmooth rock
Snarls and grunts rip the hiss of the sea
Scattered boulders sun-stiffened like blood clots
On the shore's smooth blade before the trees

Snow flak

Speeding but our car seems at a standstill,
Boring down a wind tunnel of black
Through black, in the headlights whiteness
Whirls, snow flak from unseen guns
Far below the autobahn's tarmac

You can imagine this the cockpit
Of some bomber en route through night
And blizzards to the Ruhr and its flak towers
You can imagine it – to a point.
Where is the bucking aircraft floor
The skull banged against the bomber's ribs
The holes punched through, the terror
That grips time fast with whitened knuckles
You can imagine imagination's accessories
Figment it stark and terrible as you like,
Stink of blood, nerves like toothache,
A buddy whose burst skin discloses the same stuff
As the butcher's cleaver cleaves asunder
Imagine what you will
Maybe a finer kind of cliché,
Cinematic particles
Feeding imagination's hunger
No, it's just

A cold-filled old car
On an empty autobahn,
Hastening back to Essen,
Just ahead of the real storm
In nineteen seventy-nine
Isn't that enough?

On the Grand Canal
near Suchow

Along the canal
Clumps of water hyacinth
Nod in sinusoidal sequence
To greet our barge's bow-wave

In a Farm-Worker's House at Che-chiang, near Wuhan

Cradling one of his kittens I asked
'What makes the air in here so fragrant?'
The guide: 'He says it's their natural smell'

Preparations for a 35th Birthday

Peking

An army truck trundles ahead of our coach
Along the broad avenue leading to the square
Bringing into the city a detachment of salvias –
Red flowers, green leaves – and as we approach,
My eye catches, amidst the trembling flowers,
Soldiers in green, too, with scarlet patches at cap and
throat.
Through the coach windscreen
Smiles are exchanged with the martial gardeners
Looking back over their tailgate

The ten thousand flagstones, each with its own
Plimsoll-scuffed number painted on,
Will serve again this October as stations
For the saluting beneath their sunlike leaders
Looking down from the Gate of Heaven.
Even now, down all the avenues, the potted plants
Wait patiently where deposited,
Perfect floral comrades

Hs'ian

Near the mound of the first emperor
Sagging lines of pottery soldiers
Stare dully, clay from clay at clay;
Amid shuffling locals in hideous mud-stained garb
Fat-arsed foreigners in romper suits
Snout their cameras
Squeal pink & yellow

$\rightarrow$

Hangchow

Sober tea-bushes corduroy the slopes
                                   Oolong, meaning
Rice tufts stitch the reflective paddy fields
                                   Black dragon

Emperor Le's Second Death

Thirteen emperors are buried within this valley
Around its green slopes their tombs perch high
From our vantage point we pick them out
One by one, dwarfed and blurred by distance,
Giant beehives painted smoky imperial red.

We stand around in the cedar-pillared funeral hall
Where once the spectral third emperor of the Ming
Had sat invisibly enthroned to receive yearly rites.

Glass cases now crowd the hall, holding spoil
From the despoiled tomb of another dead emperor.
Our guide with darting fingers points to photographs
In awful black-and-white of the opened tomb –
A skull and a broken trail of vertebrae caterpillared
Over a sordid tangle of rags that were silk.

'We knew nothing them,' explained the guide
'The air we let in when the tomb was opened
Destroyed his flesh instantly.'
So the emperor fled.

Perhaps up until that moment he had been alive
In a strange way, enjoying his riches and concubines.
Pick pierced the mound, a heavy stone fell in
And he perished for the second time.

$\rightarrow$

We gaze at a queen's crown on display there
A hard bonnet of woven gold
Mounted with pale blue dragons;
At long gowns of heavy silk
Embroidered with phoenix, clouds and dragons,
Knowing now that up behind this hall is
The tumulus, a green and pineclad mound,
Unopened, unpierced, its hidden entrance
Undiscovered, and in it, deep underground,
The third emperor and all his panoply
Keep ghostly court in an earthy cocoon.

We stroll back down, back to the coach,
And then, against the threshold of the triple gate
Resting in the dust, blown against its half-inch step
A black-and-white butterfly has alighted.
My shadow fails to move it, nor my breath.
In my hand I hold a doubled cloisonné
Of chequered cells, black and white.
I turn him over. All his arms folded
Across his chest, his antennae motionless
His proboscis like a coiled watch spring
His great blue and gold eyes remind me
Of the two queens' crowns, bulbous helmets
But here blue mesh tricked with gold.

I slip him into an empty cigarette
Packet and bring him away with me
This black-and-white Emperor
From Chang Ling tomb.

Templum

There are two of us it seems
                    Polar mansion
One, the greatest of the emperors
Who sits fast at the centre of his square palace
                    Square within square
All astride the sun's meridian.

                    His throne the middle square
His ears hearken unto the east and west
                    Of the nine-square, itself a square
His eyes gaze southwards to the sun

                    Within square within square
Down the only path that he can ever take

And then me, a tattered wanderer,
Haunter of the endless roads of the empire
By Canton I dreamt I was a bird of fire
Off Shanghai I rolled my blue scales in the sea
Above Lhasa crouched like a tiger in the snow
On the Wall clashed my black armour
Bending my head as the Mongol winds blow.

The dragon moves off his node
Before break of day with all his retinue
Has passed through the gate in the cinnabar walls
Through the wintered city, close-shuttered.
Drums booming, flags cracking, down the sacred road
At the round temple to sacrifice and to pray
To heaven which grants him all he has to own
So too must the poor man halt a while
Abandon motion, unfold his mat and alone
Kneel before some convenient pile
Of rocks and let the midday sun warm his face

Acts of Impiety

'I'm sorry to have to tell you your father's died.'
I was twenty-one. I said 'Thank you' and shut the door.
My friends I comforted as best I could with a light word,
Phoned for the train times and set off home.
I ate a good lunch in the restaurant car, with wine,
Fell into conversation with a friendly middle-aged man.
'Home, actually. My father's just died,'
I said, and saw him blench.

At the undertakers we, mainly I, bargained hard,
Bought the plainest coffin – it'd burn anyway,
Questioned the man about how cremation works.
At the registrar's wondered how the ordinary man copes.

We heard an uncle threw up when he heard the news,
And he and his wife cried loudly at the service
Where they played 'Jerusalem' a hymn I thought he'd liked.
And we'd had a drink or two at the pub beforehand
As the house with all the relatives was too funereal,
And afterwards I hung my new suit away.

I said I'd pick up the ashes in their cardboard box
And scatter them in the park where they used to walk
But I never got round to it

And in Babylon the unfed ghosts roamed the streets,
Lost, wailing like owls, and eating the refuse,
And drinking standing water – but these were the ghosts,
It is said, of those who had no children

A Fugue on Two Themes

Between cool sheets we lie parallel
A night breeze blows through the open shutters
Outside, I know, a full moon rides high
And restless dogs roam the silent town
Waves pant and whisper on the beach
Now you stand in silhouette against the white
Night sky, in thought, fingering your lip
In imagination or reality it doesn't matter
I followed you down the compulsive steps
To the shore, watched you watching the black
Waves mounting ever upwards – then,

I would have said, a triton rolled a fat belly
In the shallows, grinned and spread webby arms,
Clasped in which you tumbled into the deep.

And at breakfast we planned an excursion
And I did not say how your perfume tanged of brine.

From the Weissenburger Strasse: I

How can I watch the birds fly
And not want to go with them

Planes fly by my window
All day and into the night

Planes growl across the sky in my window
Tomorrow I will sit and be sad
Seeing one with a red tail taking you away

His lips on yours, his hands on your body
The way you smile when you speak of him
Razors that slice into my heart

To hope that one day I might cross
The enormous room towards your eyes
Again feel your arms around my neck

From the Weissenburger Strasse: II

Together we ate figs in the garden
Then I had to go; on my return
Latched was the wicker-gate, and you
Standing under the tree bare-breasted
Held up a snake for me to see
It won't bite, you said, and held it fast
Open the gate, open the gate, and let me in
You shook your head and the snake smiled

From the Weissenburger Strasse: III

You have misused your power
You have travelled and not seen
You have never lived the hour
Preferred will be to what has been
When you needed it your spear has failed you
When you needed it you dropped your shield
You have never known what it is that ails you
Nor on whose behalf you your power wield
Stand up straight and bow yourself down
See more clearly but with one eye closed
Kill yourself daily to be reborn

From the Weissenburger Strasse: IV

He is not the black spectre of whom I dreamed
Not someone to fear or someone to maim
He is not the man who wrecked what seemed
So finally achieved – no, someone the same
As me, with head and heart, afraid too

From the Weissenburger Strasse: V

Lying close to you
A boat rocking on the sea
My hand trailing in the water
Kissed by a wave

Two Crows

Like wet black rags
Two crows flap through river mist
As thick as milk
If there were wind
The willows would rattle their branches

The Lesson

As if an older man should slip into
The youngster's bed
Thrust him aside
Saying look this is how you do it
Guiding his hand
That is how you can give pleasure
Rein in and apply the spur
And at length the girl
On her back in the lilac sheets
Bridges up her spine and
Wilfully bumps him away
Reaching a slim hand to the boy
Come she says softly
Your way I prefer
Clumsy and inexpert, but honest
and from a full heart

Not Sentimental

Even I accompany death on her rounds
As with swift and unexpected dart
Her soft mouth whips out from grassy cover
Some small and squirming creature.
Sometimes they get one last chance
But if wing is broken, or haunches lamed,
Then must I be death's henchman,
With my bare hands or hard boot heel
Sending off vole or shrew, rabbit or pigeon,
To its particular underworld.

Some survive - the heroic mole removed
Chittering with anger from my dog's jaws,
Like a warm grey purse heavy with coin,
A gold drop of urine on the end of his prick
And walking away I reflected that even a mole
Has a voice

The Invasion of Britain

Approaching fifty, I begin to see
What the dark wood could be
Interlaced and tangled bough and branch ...

Maybe Cassivellaunus was about my age,
Approaching fifty, when he passed out the word
For the farmers to bring in cattle and families,
For the men to take farm tools to the smiths
But to save their axes for the work in the woods.

Of course, he knew the Romans would win in the end,
The round houses and cellular fields yoked, so to speak,
Beneath their four-square cities, the people killed by peace.

Approaching fifty, sometimes I stop still and realize
That once again I have escaped the Romans, for a while.

Grown from Japanese Soil

Skywriting in black letters too distant to read
Autumn geese swoop down one after the other
Cuneiform in the cold sands of the estuary beach

In Kyoto flowering reeds imitate snow falling
Clattering feathers shake in the setting sun

A Wider Ocean

No need to call home to get my news –
Behind the house the willowherb will be
Floating purple on the summer grass
A string of pheasant chicks scooting along the hedgerow,
Beneath the ash in my garden corner
The foxgloves towering in the gloom.
There will be ragwort to be pulled in the paddock
And the kestrel as usual high
On the telegraph wire
In the pasture across the lane

The fallow deer step cautiously out of the wood
The owls sleep in the trees
The woodpeckers whoop like howler monkeys

I never expected to so miss my old house
Listening in a small town in county Clare
To the song of a quavering old woman
And a soft tin whistle like wind in the reeds
Here they still mourn their people who
Had to cross a wider ocean

Dea Abscondita

In your precincts cold water drips on stone
Amongst fallen columns and brambles
A tethered old horse grazes.

Where is the darkness and the flames?
The pulse and thud of drums and chanting?
The sudden shocking flow of blood and the white
Flash of her teeth in her ecstasy?

Perhaps it is the times we live in
Which make priestesses into mere women
And women into crop-haired prisoners
In a new compound of the mens' camp.
And everyone is made into everything
So that everyone is the same as everyone else –
So long as there is one hand to put
Money in the pocket and another to take it out.

Were I, for example, to dial your particular number,
Is your voice on the machine a fading recollection of
another age?
Are you long gone away, does your house stand empty?
Perhaps you too now prefer couch and television
When the phone rings

Alta Marina

Late late in the afternoon
When the sun is westering homeward
We three lie shadowclad under the cherry laurel
Enjoying the coolness of the sun's lee
Wafted by breezes

Our triple company can boast
Ten legs, two tails, lives eleven,
Five eyes (the cat lost one of his), two sexes

This is the time when the house, cool at midday,
Has become too warm and the harshness of the day
outside
Softens down and indoors is too gloomy

The date palm, storm-tilted, rattles its fronds
Swallows shriek in swung curves, guard dogs bark
The buzzsaw noise of boys on motorbikes
The regular grind of the breeze-block factory
For once, as I write, form part of a harmony
And even a car overrevving cannot make a bum note
Nor the shuddering climactic grief of the donkey

One-eyed cat, black dog and me
Lying prone on the dead grass with lazy flies
In my yard by my house beneath a tree
One thinking: How many years between us?
As like three planets orbiting the same sun
My dog making seven full revolutions
For each of mine, the cat perhaps four

The House in Xaló

My cat sits in the sun
Like a bottle on the gravel

Overhead the swallows scream
Like blades cutting
Arcs in the sky

The cat jumps
Claws out
For a moment
Hangs magnificently
Extended in the air

As if I were to spring fifteen foot
Straight up
From my deckchair

He only has one eye
Cannot benefit from parallax
Doesn't know
The swallows are laughably out of reach

Not like me
Knowing better
Who have two
And would not jump

A Poet Recently Deceased

Illicitly at night under sheet and blankets
The boy roams the white countries of the page
With torch and fearless curiosity
Taking his own immortality for granted
Death, pain and loss if not completely unknown
Then at least healing quickly
Out there in the white world meeting the great makers
Listening to them, honouring them
With the years becoming one of their number
Becoming acquainted with disease, loss and
Mortal pleasures in the coloured world
But singing with ever stronger voice
Clear water from a strong fountain
And immortal in the white world
Until outside all the colours fall to black
And even sounds are muted

And in the hospital bed a white-bearded old man
Insists to his young self that he is still immortal
And that he still has so much to say
And yet it is perhaps an indulgence
An inaccuracy to speak of tragedy.
The bed you lie in, those sheets you spread
Sympathy for someone brought down
Repeatedly by fatal flaws (like my own).
In one pan of the balance, the works,
The other holds a stack of iron weights
Variously labelled, variously heavy
Which grows like a compact ziggurat

$\rightarrow$

As my acquaintanceship of the poems deepens
I know you drink, frequently, possibly to excess
By own admission cigarettes by the score each day
This the one side of an equation, the other, I suspect,
The twelve disastrous fires,
Then your boom and bust cycle of plenty and penury
Prosecution in the 60s for not paying contributions:
At forty you condemn your eighty-year-old self
To being refused pensions and medical treatment from the
state

Once again your friends will rally round
On the face of it you only have yourself to thank

I judge you harshly
As one treading a similar road
Which must end somewhere across the horizon
In the pitch darkness
Now encompassing you

Zoology

If cats are owls
Dogs must be parrots
But, for some reason
Of their own, ungaudy.

The Hill Farm

Rusty barbed wire binds the gate closed
The ruts up to the old house and barn
Slip away slowly into rank grass and bushes
An abandoned habitation harboured
Within toppling walls of mottled stones.
On the grassy oceans outside them
Unnumbered sheep bob chewing.
High above the windy hills buzzards'
Calls claw curves into the sky
A crow cronks leaving a bare oak

Once an unmarried farmer lived here
With his ma. She died.
Years later, the door broken in,
Him they bumped down the stairs
And presently all the hundreds of dead bottles.

It is easy to imagine him still lying up there,
Helpless behind the blank window-holes
In the house which never will be up for sale
Until it is finally unoccupied

An Attempt at Empathy

I wonder what would happen
If I tried to climb in those windows.
When his dad died, did that tie him
Fast to his mother? Was it too late
For him to find a wife, to marry?
Who would take on his widowed mother?
The cat-fighting of women in that dark house.
What does he see when he looks out?
The meaningless greenness, the sheep,
Their droppings like bits of liquorice.
Long featureless days of visiting the flocks,
Taking out hay bales in February,
Then fighting the crows for the lambs.
Night confronts him with himself.
The shadows in the farmhouse mutter,
Then nag, then scream at him.
What solution does the whiskey bring?
Every evening giving in.
More than an hour's walk downhill
Down the lane to the village.
The usual purchase, friendly smile at the till
Of someone trying not to judge,
But still *thinking*.
He knows what he, what they are all thinking.
Slowly uphill, sitting from time to time
On a wall, a little pull from the bottle.
Hauling his middle-aged bulk back home
In a night swig by swig less threatening,
More cosy, like the navy-blue woollen blanket
Which eventually slides off the bed
To awake you to another merciless dawn.

Nightmare in a Clarksdale Motel

The crossroads is deserted
The traffic lights bounce on the wires
Trees shudder as the night wind strokes them
My shirt flaps, cold sweat on my chest

Someone seems to be standing
Beside the telegraph pole
Bulky, big-shouldered in dark clothes
White flecks are his eyes

This is the crossroads
The real one
In the dead town's backstreets
By the old railroad track
So I know who it has to be

Reality is a card which always turns up different

I expected, if anyone, a dangerously
Dapper Baron Samedi, sardonically
Smiling, diamonds on his fingers,
Not this sad hulk with reproachful eyes
I'm not here, I realize, to do a deal

I'm not here to trade my soul
For a demonic injection of unearthly power
That's not what is going to happen.
No, it appears I've turned up to apologize
For letting him down, yet again

He doesn't speak, just gazes
It's a personal matter between me and him
Although it's the first time I've seen him
Somehow I've been here countless times before

$\rightarrow$

When I speak, he doesn't answer
I find I really have nothing to say
He just waits, gazes, doesn't move

Now I lie in my motel room
Seeing him still
And it's always me who first walks away

Civilian Casualties

There's been a mouse in the pantry
I've seen him a few times
In his field-grey fur
Frozen by sudden light.
He hasn't found the food yet,
Has had to manage on magazine
Covers and starch in book spines.
The humane trap he raids
And somehow never gets caught.

I tolerate these small incursions,
He has his job to do as I mine.
Now he's pushed it a bit too far
(In my view) whiskering out
Into the kitchen at night
And chewing ragged mushy holes
In the potatoes – perhaps he's starving

Outside the buzzards may wheel
High above the oaks
Unlike his kind in the bare grass
He has no need to fear them

One morning I come downstairs
There's a strange dark shape in the sink
Where a pan is soaking.
He's pawing desperately the
Unforgiving steep sides of the sink.

Saved in a pan he is bright-eyed, sleek,
Seemingly tolerant of my touch,
Like a rescued torpedoed sailor.
I put him in dry cloth in a box
To dry out before I release him in the barn.

$\longrightarrow$

Driving back home later from an errand
I see in the verge something cat-sized,
Strangely hobbling –
A flash of yellow beak and a proud eye.
To my relief the downed buzzard pushes
Through the hedge and into the glade
Where his mate is calling.

At home I check on the mouse –
He's under the cloth, but on his back,
Convulsing, pink paws clasping and
Unclasping as the washing-up liquid
Burns through his innards.
Meanwhile a Land Rover on the hill
Squashes the wounded buzzard
Into a sordid mess of broken umbrellas.

Sheet Music

We lie a while naked on the white sheets
Now rumpled and damp. It's
Three a.m. in a Bangkok hôtel room.

With fingers delicate but strong
I caress her neck.
She, shining black, sits
On one thigh, leans against my other.
My freer right hand,
My male hand, the stronger hand,
Moves back and forth,
Brushing, tickling,
Sometimes hard, sometimes soft.
From its curves her body sings,
A body I bought a few hours before
For a handful of notes.

In this year, on this visit,
I am two decades older,
A regular drinker of my shame,
And find myself once again
In a Bangkok hôtel room –
But not like last time,
With some poor girl from the bars.
No, this time, with a new guitar.

Afterwards I write these words
On a sheet of ruled staves.
The pen moves up and down,
Inking the white paper,
And another way of making love
Is consummated on the page

The Dream

In dreams I meet you
In dreams last night I saw you
Playing Queen Gertrude's lady-in-waiting
Your black hair falling heavy as jet
Kohl-rimmed eyes flashing white.
Later you allowed me to hold you
In my arms and we conversed softly
In the dream's dream-world.

In fact you died ten years ago –
In that world I slowly forget you
Until I dream in the dream's dream-world
And find you again.

Now we're riding a wide shallow boat
On the green river. It overturns.
Something is lost in the water.
Your laughter like jewels of spray.
The boat is gone, the water cool.
Swimming I awake – or do I fall
Asleep or have I drowned?

Must I wait to die
To be with you always?
Could you die in that world too
As you died in this?

The Blackbird

Rain on the roof
Sounds sift through onto my bed
Outside my window
Water drops spatter the bushes
And a blackbird sings
In the late dusk of June

Inside, the blackbird in the thorntree
In the painting on my wall
Listens with his yellow eye
And further away on the canvas plain
White-blazed gemsbok lift their heads

Last year I saw *this* blackbird
In *this* tree by a track in Hluhluwe
(Just before the elephants crossed)
Exactly as prophesied
By an unknown painter in Suffolk
Some years before

The painted landscape
Swirls down the blackbird's eye.
In hyperspace, twenty-four planes
Spin around the thread
Joining his eye and mine

The Nymphs

On a radiator shelf in the junk shop
The very tiniest dolls clothes
Are casually displayed for sale

A crimson skirt of silk
Crumpled on the cool marble
And a couple of purple blouses perhaps

A double-take solves the puzzle:
Petals from sweet peas in a jam jar
And dropped in haste
By naked dancers
Departing

Before Words

Before language and locomotion,
Nothing came to me clothed -
Coal dust in the air, fog rasping the throat,
In summer, the smell of rain on pavements;
At all seasons rubbery odours from the gasworks,
Smoke from the black locomotives,
The electric smell of our coal shed,
The thump in the air as an express hurtles through
Up on the embankment
At the end of our shadowed garden.
Clinking of distant shunting,
Snarl of Brown's saw mill.
''Arry!' yelled in the builder's yard next door
''Arry!' from my pram under the apple tree.
Clumps of cat pee in the sandbox,
The horror of a whiskery tramp at the gate.
The town-hall clock walks up and down its chimes
And then slowly gongs out the afternoon hour

Harpocrates

In the grey marshland
Birds clatter from under my feet
In flashes of heart in the mouth.
Through water thick with dead reed

Reaching the navel copse of alders
I clambered up wobbly tussocks of grass
To a silence and an air of vacancy,
Like hearing voices but opening the door
On an empty room

Under a stunted tree
A toppled stone the size of a child,
Its face almost hidden under moss.
My forefinger ploughs free
The clogged grooves
And then I heave it upright,
Rocking it back into its old socket

Eyes opened
There was speaking
Without use of lips.
At nightfall
I left like a sleepwalker

Poems
from
Poems

Semez la graine

Sow the grain, sow the grain
In my former gardens

And I'm speaking of the living ideal siren
      Mistress of the spume and the night harvests
      Where swirling constellations spill out
      A thunder of periwinkles and daisies

We're off to Lisbon

Soul heavy, heart light
To gather belladonna
In my former gardens

And I'm speaking of the ideal living siren

      Not a figurehead, but a figure of flesh
      Living, insatiable
      No-one will forgive you

Heavy soul, heart light

Siren of Lisbon
Tawny lioness of the bright eyes

And I'm speaking of the living ideal siren

      Once upon a time
      A siren lived in Lisbon

Sow the grain, sow the grain
In my former gardens

      Lisbon flowersmoke

      We're off to Lisbon
      Soul heavy, heart light
      No-one will forgive you
      Tawny lioness of the bright eyes   →

Sow the grain, sow the grain

Once I knew the song
The siren sang
Beneath the house

We're off to Lisbon

Soul heavy, heart light
To gather belladonna
In my former gardens

Very black midnight

The night every flower
Pour and drink, pour and drink
Is the same colour

Once I knew the siren

Once I knew her song
See her dress trail
See it charm the fishes

But the spouting grain
Knows not its flower

To each day its terminus
To each love its sorrows

Liana Fountain

Waves break upon a beach
Foliage breaks upon the sky
Spray   buds

Silver lianas festoon these trees
Trunks weather-gnarled
Fresh is the forest
Light plays upon a spring
Water droplets   clash of diamonds

An adolescent sprawls in the fountain
Grey eyes in a pale face
Perchance he dreams

                    of gilded seas

Red-beaked bird sips and bathes
Spreads wings in the sunlight

                    of palm trees

Lady's fan reflects the sun

                    maybe, even, of a girl

Jungle

Black velvet panther
Steel spring muscles
Sleeps elegantly

Gazelles move fastidiously in the dark
Night breeze   pool ripples   lotus bobs
Animal scent seduces his nostrils

Panther slips into shadows
Distant scream

Ravine

Bamboo gorge   shadow-filled
Eye of the sun   cannot meet it
Midday's awkward   silence

Hardened lava-flows   scab on a deep scar

Freshets   disappear in white gravel
Innumerable   hard white suns
Colibri beetles   ricochet
Birds flowers insects   in profusion

Technicolour   lizard on warm rock
Emerald back   glints in the sun
Half-closed eyes   amber slits

Elephants Having Crossed A Desert

Red savannah   lions doze
Boa   tessellated enamel   hangs in tree
Birds' wings   claw through thick air

Red dusted   elephants
Ears flap   eyes screwed up
Acrid sweat   insect clouds

Leathery beads
On an invisible wire
Come and are gone

Desert

Oasis palms
Dusty shadows
Shrivelled dates

Desert moon
Campfire circle
Murmur of camelmen

Far dunes
Jackal's yelp
Camels stir in their sleep

At Ships With Tattooed Sails

Seaweed rots on an arid beach
Stench of horse and cow bones
Skinny mongrels howl feverishly

Mute world, too dull for anger
Dead world, effects lacking executor
Solitary moon in a bilious sky

Black waves lap the
Black sand
        without interest

Lee Shore

Ancient rocks tumbled on the beach
Hang in black silt
Heave of the sea swell
Rolling over the submerged stars

Catullus XLVII

Porcius and Socration, greed and cunning,
You two thieving left hands of Governor Piso,
(Whom Cicero had a go at for embezzlement)
You palm-itching mange upon the world,
The circumcised Priapus himself prefers you
To my friends Fabullus and Veraniolus,
Who both grew lean in Piso's service.
Expense and honest work alike have
No meaning for you and your oh so elegant,
Oh so sophisticated banquets.

You see *my* friends hanging about the streets
To catch your invitations?

Catullus LII

Why don't you die, Catullus? What else remains?
Nonius Strumus – meaning pus-boil – sits on the Senate;
Vatinius fakes votes for the presidential elections.
Why not die, Catullus? What else remains?

Catullus LIII

Some guy in the crowd made me laugh.
When my Calvus had itemized all his accusations
Against Vatinius, wonderfully.
With adoration this guy raises his fist
'Right on! The little sod's an orator!'

Sources

Robert Desnos

Semez la graine from 'Siramour' in the *Fortunes* collection (NRF, 1969)

Leconte de Lisle

All from the *Poèmes Choisis* collection, ed. Eggli (Univ. Manchester, 1943)

Liana Fountain from *La Fontaine aux Lianes*
Jungle   from *Les Jungles*
Ravine   from *La Ravine Saint-Gilles*
Elephants...   from *Les Éléphants*
Desert   from *Le Désert*
At Ships...   from *Les Hurleurs*

Stories

Grafting in Birkenhead

You stood up from your desk in front of the window, pushing the chair back with the back of your knees. You pushed your fingers back through your hair, and then sniffed them to see if your hair needed washing yet. You pushed the knot of your tie up into place, and then strolled outside for a smoke. You rolled a cigarette, lighted it and took a long drag, with your bum resting comfortably on the windowsill. 'No Matches or Inflammable Articles to be brought into this Refinery' in red letters. Underneath that, a double column of closely printed and carefully numbered regulations, headed by the black capitals 'FIRE REGULATIONS'. The other sign, white letters on a chipped and rusting blue enamel rectangle, said simply 'STOP HERE'.

You glanced at your watch, and then you turned and stuck your head in through the open office window to check the time by the big old railway clock on the wall. It read a little before a quarter to ten.

To your left, up an approach road, walled in one both sides by ten feet of concrete topped by three strands of barbed wire. At the end of it, the city. A road one hundred and fifty feet long leading to life and noise. A road which led to the main road you drove along every morning at seven thirty on your way to work. You came out of the Mersey Tunnel and turned left and south, passing by the Cammell-Laird shipyards, the rust-brown slums and the dusty terraces of empty shops. Then you turned down into this road, past the sign which says 'SHELL-MEX OIL REFINERY SLOW'.

Your mate in the checkpoint office, old Podger, just finishing his night shift, would be swinging back the wire mesh gates for your car. He'd go back inside without waiting, fold up the tired evening paper, and put it into the old oily gas-mask case together with his empty bait tin.

You could smell his smell as you entered the warm stuffiness of the room, which was slipping out fast through the open door into the nippiness of the morning.

Now alone, you put on your police jacket, and sat down for the next eight hours of collecting matches and lighters; making tea; reading the paper; watching people, oilmen and seamen, coming and going. Cushy job for an old cop.

The old green land rover with as usual three men in it – well, one man and two lads – squashed into the cab, pulled to a stop outside the office for the third morning now.

'Lookit the lazy bastard,' said Phil the driver, jerking his thumb at the cop standing smoking his rolly. The cop grinned and waved lazily, and the two lads waved back, grinning at Phil's continual muttered undercurrent of obscenities.

'Morning!' cried Phil. 'Lazy bastard sitting on his fat arse.'

'Here again?' said the cop.

'That's right. We can't keep away.'

'Got any matches for me, son?'

'Not just yet. We're gonna have a quick smoke before we go in.'

'Okay, lad. That's what I allus do so as I'm – '

'Well, we'll bring 'em over when we're ready.'

The cop took the hint and ambled back to his windowsill. Phil shot a quick glance at the two lads.

'They're all bloody dozy those cops, all on 'em, can't do bugger all 'cept sit on their fat arses all day... dozy sods, all on 'em... and they're all as bent as nine-bob notes into the bargain... bastards.'

Phil looked up from his muttering over his rolly to meet the boys' smiles. He smiled back; he knew they lapped it up, and even encouraged him.

After some minutes Tom, the older of the two brothers, spoke up.

'Are we having tea first, Phil?'

'Oh, yeah. Course. I reckon we can spare ten minutes like for a quick brew-up. Bloody well hope so. That's all that dozy sod Martin does at the yard all day... bloody di-rector. Him and his Triumph fooking Stag, and his beer gut, and his lah-de-dah secretary. I should think we could. I should think we could. Here, use my can anyway, la.'

Tom slid out of the cab, and went to fish Phil's tea can out of the trailer. Joe shifted across to the window from his uncomfortable position above the transmission and slid down in the seat so his knees touched the dash while he looked vacantly out.

'Hey, Phil, how many more days have we got coming to this dump, eh?'

'Fed up already?'

'No, not really. I just wondered, that's all. Doesn't seem as big as Eastham though, and we did that in two days.'

'Another two days here and we'll be through. There's those tanks over by... d'you see, by that dock effort. And then those big bastards over there. Then we got it all wrapped up.'

'So why couldn't we do it today then?'

Phil frowned, thought briefly and then replied slyly.

'It's possible, like. But you don't want to bust a gut, do you? I mean, specially for those lazy sods back at the yard. No, I reckon we'll give ourselves two days, nice and easy like. Not skiving, mind... but not shagging ourselves neither.'

Phil grunted as he licked the paper, and turning the fag around in his big hand, regarded it with satisfaction. He passed the tobacco tin over to Joe, who hadn't been thinking about cigarettes.

'Cheers.'

There was a brief silence, during which Phil scratched himself carefully through his trousers. He rubbed his nose and spoke.

'How's yer brother enjoying it, kid? He's not thinking of jacking it in, is he? I'd rather work with him and you than all those old slobs like Sherb and Rog. They're fook all. You know, old and slow. They're past it. They're past real graft. And they're lazy. And stupid, like. They're always going the wrong fooking way, or tripping you up, or, you know, I dunno, they ought to be pensioned off or something. I tell you, if either of you two leaves, I'm gonna quit as well. Find something else to do. I just can't stand the idea of having to be with that slob Sherb farting and belching all day.'

'No, I don't think he'll leave,' Joe said. 'In fact, I think he enjoys it. He says he doesn't have to think.'

Phil stared out of the window as if he didn't understand, as if he was shocked, maybe.

'Booger me,' he said finally. 'You know, lad, if I had his chances, I wouldn't fooking be here. Education, that's meant to be used. I mean, that's what it's for, innit? Don't think I enjoy this sodding job, lad, cos I don't. It's okay tooling around if you're not married. It's either this or blooming Courtaulds. Look, take my advice, lad, use your brains and get somewhere. And you can tell that to yer brother.'

Joe smirked to himself. The 'get on, lad' was such a pure Northern cliché, but it obviously meant something to Phil, which meant he had to take it a bit more seriously himself. Tom loped back, swinging the tea can, and set it on the flat bonnet of the land rover. He walked past the window whistling and disappeared to put on his wellies.

Phil winked at Joe.

'That bloody tea ready yet, Tom? Your kid's dying for some.'

'Half a tick,' came the reply. 'Gotta brew. Pass out your mugs and I'll be mummy.'

'Daft sod,' said Phil.

'Here come da heat,' Joe said with a grin.

The cop reappeared with his old tea-stained china mug.

'Oh, that soft booger's giving him our tea. You can't help but laugh, can you.'

Ten minutes later, after drinking tea with the lad, you took in their matches and let them into the refinery for the morning. If yesterday was anything to go by, you wouldn't see them again until eleven, their tea break. Then they wouldn't reappear until their dinner hour. Then they'd be in all afternoon, except for ten minutes around three o'clock – all afternoon until seven or even later.

They were driving slowly along one of the service roads, the funnel of the spark guard shoved into the exhaust. On their left, and stretching ahead to the perimeter fence, were the storage tanks. Each group of four stood in a flat area called the compound. The ground there was covered with chips of grey stone, and surrounded by ten-foot grass banks. They were supposed to contain all the oil that would be released if the tanks burst for any reason. Predominant colour of tanks, pipes, ground, sky: pale blue-grey. Every tank, all the miles of thick pipe and thin pipe, every valve was painted this colour. High up on its side, each tank bore a black number. Each pipe too had its number and code (which expressed its contents). On their right, more tanks and pipes. Alongside the service road ran the thin red water pipes and every so often the red plates of the hydrant point.

They stopped right by one of these hydrant points. Tom jumped down from the back. Phil and Joe opened the doors and got out. Nobody spoke.

Tom took the thick iron road from out of the trailer and used it to prise open the heavy cast-iron lid of the hydrant, forcing it back and over with his foot. Down inside, in the wet blackness, were the two rusted nozzles of the hydrant. Joe had dragged the key across. This was a long and heavy implement shaped like a tall T. The bottom few inches were thicker, and a cubic hole had been made in its base. Joe fitted this over one of the square 'taps' in the hydrant.

Tom returned, dragging the brass end of the canvas hose. This he screwed over one of the nozzles. Right now, the hose was flat, like a flattened-out straw. While the two boys were doing this, Phil took off the round lid of the tank on the back of the land rover. He pushed his end of the hose into the tank and signalled to Tom to turn on the hydrant. The hose suddenly distended along its length, and gallons of water under pressure surged into the tank. The hose pulsed as if it were alive – like some mechanical equivalent of an artery.

Next they had to prepare the herbicide. They were using a mixture: some solid stuff plus a measure of Paraquat, which was a poison with no known antidote. It can attack the eyes, so great care was needed not to splash any. While Tom prepared the mix, Phil was telling Joe a story.

'...well, it was when we were at this caper last year – you remember that new part of Stanlow – you know, where you go through the village, and sort of round the back into the site. Well, last year there was this dozy old twat on the gate, you know the type, well, he was a real nosy old git and was always asking questions like and on the scrounge. Anyway he kept asking me about what he should put on his fooking lawn – he'd kept his lawn like a bowling green – dead flat and no weeds allowed, except he couldn't get rid of this fooking dandelion. So he asks me every morning till finally I gives him some Paraquat. I says be careful with it, mind, and he nods and says he will. So I gives him a little bottle of it like. We're off then for two weeks on those leccy substations and when I gets back to Stanlow and sees this old git, well, he goes fooking mad, all red in the face and shouting and carrying on like. So I says 'Look calm, down, you know, I mean, what's up?' and he says to me, and I nearly split a gut trying not to laugh, he says 'Your fooking weedkiller'. I says 'What about it? It worked didn't it?'

'Worked?' he says. 'Worked? It worked too fooking well! It's killed off my whole fooking lawn, that's how it worked! I took sixteen years,' he says, still shouting like, 'Sixteen years to get it like that' and he went on and on and on – and I had to drive in and I just sits and laughs and laughs and laughs.'

Joe laughed with Phil, but he felt sorry for the old boy.

'It'll wash out with the rain, though, won't it, Phil?'

Phil stared at him as if he were one of those types who don't understand the punchline of a good joke.

'Oh, aye, lad,' he replied, and then with a guffaw: 'But not for another twenty years. I'd had to tell the missus...'

Tom heard the main part of the story as he poured the oil drum full of the mix into the tank. He could see the old man's face with tears on it. The story was typical of Phil, there was a sort of blindness in him. He wasn't stupid by any means but the times when Tom accidently caught his gaze he couldn't help but think that his eyes had the dumb glazed look of an animal's.

'Let's gerron then,' said Phil. 'Ready, Tom?'

Tom nodded and they all got back into or onto the land rover. Phil drove to the turning point where they backed up the trailer and uncoupled it. Joe and Tom prepared the thin rubber hose. One end screwed into the tank and then Phil drove off at a speed just faster than walking pace while Tom and Joe carefully uncoiled its five or six hundred feet, making sure it didn't kink, until it lay extended flat and true behind the land rover. Then Joe was left holding just the brass lance. He raised his arm and the land rover stopped. Then they walked up through the dust, with the hose doubling behind them, the loop following them and collecting an ever-increasing load of twigs and dust in its bight.

'Here we go,' said Joe as the note of the engine changed and they knew it was now working the pump.

'I'll be glad when it's seven,' Joe added unnecessarily.

Tom squeezed the handle of the lance and a fine jet of herbicide sprayed with some force into the darkening dust.

'Yeah,' Tom replied absently and gave the thumbs-up to Phil. 'What you got for lunch?'

'Sarnies and Mum's cake. You?'

'Yeah, me too. Plus soused herrings.'

Tom stressed the last two words slightly. They both knew Phil's attitude to them: 'Look like fooking snakes, they do.' And yet he would munch on tripe.

Now they had walked up as far as the land rover and Phil took the lance from Tom like a duellist takes a pistol from his second, and after muttering some instructions about pressure to Joe, ran heavy-booted down the grass bank into the compound. Joe saw Tom wait, then pick up the hose, put it over one shoulder, gripped in front and down behind by newly strong fists, and jump down after Phil, pulling the slack behind him.

Joe sat on the bonnet, thought about cigarettes, but mainly daydreamed as he watched Phil and Tom going up and down the compound floor like a two-man chain gang, covering every square inch of it with herbicide. Painting the dry grey stone wet brown. Climbing over pipes, walking along pipes, in their clumsy gumboots, silently, with heads bowed. Tom glanced behind from time to time for incipient kinks. Tom putting his back into the bight of the hose to drag five hundred feet of water-full hose over grass, pipes, gravel, around tanks and around struts. And Phil never ever being jerked up by there suddenly being not enough hose for him. Tom anticipating every turn and new direction, always having free hose lying ready for their next tank. Always seeing the small snag before the hose caught in it. And Phil never once looking over his shoulder. In perfect harmony and partnership they covered the ground relentlessly, almost as if they were rolling up carpets.

'What're you lot up to, lad?'

Joe started.

'Eh? What?'

It was an old maintenance man in oily blue overalls and with a crinkly red face.

'Eh? What're you up to?'

He pushed his face at Joe.

'Oh... killing off weeds and stuff.'

The old guy looked puzzled and then suspicious.

'I can't see any weeds like.'

'Yeah. Good, in't it?'

The red skin empurpled and began spraying indignation into Joe's face.

'Why you fooking... you fooking think you're so...'

'Take it easy, just a joke.'

'You bloody long-haired fooking layabout, you...'

The man got into his stride. Joe closed his eyes and waited for him to run out of steam. Then jab, jab, jab in the ribs and the foul breath in his face and the voice buffeting his ears. Joe could see with fascination every pore in the man's damp, pink nose. He shrugged and made to push the man away.

Then there was a shout from down in the compound.

'Oh, Christ!' said Joe. 'The bloody pressure's dropped. Look what you've made me do, you stupid old tosser.'

He pushed past the old guy and reached into the cab to shove the hand throttle up.

'Okay, lad,' came from somewhere behind the pipe racks.

Joe relaxed and looked round. The old man had quite disappeared. Joe could see unimpeded for a hundred yards in most directions, and nowhere could he see the old man.

Lunchtime in the cab outside the gates.

'How're we doing today, Phil?' asked Tom, eating a sarnie.

'Fooking All Right, la.'

Phil sounded unusually pleased. He shoved his feet forward and rolled a fag, the tin and papers on his lap.

'Two more tanks of the poison, and we've done all sixteen of those boogers. That's all the compounds this side.'

'Should finish tonight then,' said Joe, with ill-disguised enthusiasm.

'Could be, lad. Could be.'

Four o'clock and the sun going down behind the tanks. Two hours until overtime. Two more tanks to spray. Phil and Tom were on the two biggest oil tanks. Their boots crunched rhythmically on the dead gravel. The hiss of the spray and the muted noise of the traffic. Sometimes the sound of tugs towing tankers on the ship canal. Occasionally the reverberating clang-ang-ang-ng of the hose as it hits a pipe after being flicked over a strut. Neither man spoke, but kept on trudging back and forth, like automata on a sea bed.

The team was going to break up. Joe told them at tea break what they knew, that he was sick of refineries; and also what they suspected, that he would collect his cards at the end of the week. Phil was afraid of being lumbered with a fool to replace him, and Tom didn't like the idea of their efficiency as a team finished. Another person would have to be assimilated. It was good working with a brother anyway. A common front of shared humour against the imbecilic nature of the job. On the other hand, thought Tom, okay, so the refinery was dead, all gravel, concrete and metal, but there was a certain brooding ageless quality about it that he did like. There was a sort of beauty in the scores of parallel pipes rising, falling and angling in unison, the curve of shadows on the tank walls. There was even something of that in the job itself.

By the side of the compound they were working in was a

concrete trench about six feet deep. It carried three parallel three-foot crude oil pipes. At one end of the trench, by the back wall, a 'bridge' of six or seven one-foot pipes crossed over. Tom and Phil were going to use this bridge to cross over into the next compound. Joe was working behind, flicking the slack hose across in readiness. He made sure that it didn't get fouled in the puddles of oil in the trench bottom. Phil moved along the side of the trench and beckoned his next course to Joe and Tom who had naturally already sussed it out. Suddenly Phil stopped dead just by the pipe bridge, and looked carefully under it. Tom screwed up his eyes to see why. Perhaps a pipe was leaking or something. Phil seemed to beckon, so with a shrug Tom dropped the hose and walked up. Phil touched a finger to his lips, and equally meaningfully directed his chin towards the shadow.

Tom peeped over Phil's shoulder. In the shadow of the pipes was the bright face of a fox cub, shiny eyes and delicate glittering teeth, sandy-red fur. It was trembling and edging back under the sheaf of pipes. Tom held his breath and just stared in wonder at such a creature being in such a sterile unfriendly place as an oil refinery in the heart of Birkenhead. He saw Phil's teeth grinning back at him and the dullness again in his eyes. Phil turned and with a flick of the wrist sprayed the cub full in the face. The silence popped, noises returned, and the cub had disappeared. Tom stepped back and away, feeling sick.

'... fooking fox in a gofforsaken place like this,' he heard Phil's voice saying. 'Just wait til I tell the lads down the pub. Bloody rum thing, a bloody fox cub.'

'You know those lads in the refinery I was telling you about, love?' you said, dropping your gas mask case on the kitchen table. 'Well, they told me they saw a fox in the tanks today. Can you credit that? Middle of bloody Liverpool.'

'You know your trouble, don't you,' said your wife. 'You'd believe anything anyone told you, you would.'

Basement Story

The railings had been dipped into a thick emerald sauce which had dried on the rods in gouts and gobbets. The summer heat had raised blisters too, small fingers had prodded and burst them, and then picked soft rags of paint away. In other places strange local contractions of the paint skin had produced tiny ovals of crisp microscopic ripples, as sand is furrowed by the wind on a long beach. Or as when a gust of wind catspaws the liquid green.

There was a light well around the walls of the school to let light cascade down onto the high barred and dark windows of the basement. The butts of the railing spears hung a few inches above the dwarf wall of warm smooth bricks wrapped like a fireplace fender around the three open sides of the well. Elbow to elbow with his class cronies, Barry lay splay-legged, feet at twenty past eight, belly comfortable against the warm elephant skin tarmac of the playground. The boys gripped the edge of the coping stones, pushing their faces sideways through the gap beneath the railings, and peered down.

A medicinal smell of coal dust rose on the warm breath of the well, a husky breath of hot cast-iron blurred by heat, and a clanging and knocking of unseen pipes and trunking rose up to them, with the occasional grating scrape of a steel shovel jarring against concrete. The dark panes flashed orange and yellow and perhaps a shadow could be seen moving inside. Each boy gazed down isolated within his own apprehension, as when in the privacy of a bedroom the well-thumbed page is drawn back with queasy anticipation to reveal the fuzzy monochrome of an execution, with hideously distorted heads (this caused by the printing process in the ancient encyclopaedia) lying tumbled in the dust.

Down there the narrow windows were dark and begrimed, and stood slightly ajar behind their bars. The shovel scraped terribly again and made their hearts jolt. Chalky said 'He's got a tail, I bet' and Sant said 'Horns and claws as well.' There was a yellow flash and a roar from below like the flames punching out through the furnace door. They all started again.

'Let's fetch 'im out,' said Aubrey, who was Barry's cousin. A tiny pebble, a speck of stone, was tossed into the pit. There was an instant and astonishingly loud crack. 'You've gone and smashed it!' Aubrey looked frightened for a moment, but drawled 'Cracked it, possibly' in adult tones.

'Oy!' bellowed up at them from a sudden blackface with a blood-red gullet and a gin-trap of white teeth. 'Oy, you lot, clear orf!' His chest was fire-tanned, hairy and besmirched by coals, and glistened like coal dust with sweat. The voice boomed horribly in the well, and the kids jumped away and cantered off as if he were Billygoat Gruff.

Against the blanched sky of October now the looming row of sycamores dropping damp enormous leaves, and a stark run of black railings, like spears in a rack.

Every holiday the sad men in sawdust-coloured coats polished the woodblock floor in the hall and lobbies into the dark treacly gloss of a volcanic glass but only two days of children restored its usual appearance, a herringbone work of blocks of scurfy overcooked beef. Sour milk tinged the dusty air. The clock pointed to a quarter past four: the hall and its adjoining classrooms, partitioned with panels of glass above wood, echoed silence. Against a bit of real wall at the back where the brass-bound swing doors swung onto the boys' lobby (a few abandoned musty coats and scarves hung here and there on the black hooks) and their sector of playground, a broom leant with its bristles guarding a little cone of floor dustings.

Barry was perched on the edge of the stage, swinging his legs and feeling the sting where he had picked the scab from his knee. The wound was crying now and he rubbed the wet away from its astonishing fresh pork-pinkness. His father, who was deputy headmaster, was still upstairs somewhere, perhaps in the staffroom. Barry had never actually set foot in there, although he had stood at the threshold once, peeping in to see Miss Lloyd and her crimped-up hair dropping a pink cosy over the teapot. In there, he knew, they had a machine that made them tes, and told the time as well.

Heels echoed on wood and the top half of his father, who was as usual wearing his houndstooth sports jacket and dark emerald tie, moved rapidly across the gallery above the clock at the far end of the hall, from the girls' side (where appropriately enough the predominantly female staffroom was to be found) over to the boys' side and the Head's office. There was something frightening about this title: 'the Head', he knew, was also Mr Miller, who was kind and his father's friend, but who could be stern, in assembly or the time when he had caned Barry. 'The Head' also suggested some enormous version of Mr Miller's head, without arms, legs or a body, which filled his office completely. Next to the Head's room was his father's unknown chamber. 'Shan't be a tick, Barry,' he called and Barry nodded and said right-o.

As his father quit the gallery and Barry's sight at top right, the caretaker popped out at the bottom of the left-hand stairs, dithered, gave Barry a watery smile, and called out an unanswered good-bye back up the empty stairs. The school took the shout like deep cold water takes a stone. The clock ticked. Finally, his father descended, not alone and exuding a slight air of irritation but somehow still managing to be politely attendant to the harsh crow's voice of Miss Stringer, a cardiganed raw-boned spinster who liked to think that she had his ear. She, at the start of her lessons, used to snatch the children's hands up to her eyes, peer closely at them before flinging them away from her, equally disappointed it seemed whether she found dirt or cleanliness. The first meant a sharp rap of the ruler – the boys were given more edge than flat – and a trip to the lobby sink at its skin-chapping cold water and soap tablets of repellent milky-plum slime that left gobbets all over the crazed grubby porcelain. Barry kept his nails bitten to the quick, so that no crescent of dirt could clog up under them.

Miss Stringer buttoned her raincoat, from bottom to top, with fussy little twitches of her hands, and went. She wore a navy gaberdine coat with a hood and a tartan lining just like the ones her girls wore: indeed, in it she looked like nothing more than a schoolgirl hideously disfigured by age. Once she amused the boys greatly by telling them that their voices were the sweetest voices of all, 'until they spoilt' she added sourly, and then all the little girls turned round and smiled with triumph.

'Give me a hand, Barry.' His father came over from the foot of the stairs. 'There's some stuff I want bringing up,' and he waved a wad of booklets, exercise books perhaps. 'I've dug these out for you, too.' In his hand Barry recognized a good three or four of the old-style exercise books which still turned up from time to time in stockroom and store cupboard. They were covered in something that was not unlike blotting paper, with a dyed mottled look to it. Deep orange and dull lavender, and if you looked closely you could see a scatter of dark tiny fibres in the paper, like beard bristles left in the wash basin.

Barry took the copybooks and thrust them into his satchel, to trot after his father who had disappeared into a transverse wood-panelled adit which squeezed between the stage rear and the brick wall. The passage was low and windowless and smelt of dry wood, cedar. Then his father abruptly vanished sideways into a slab of inky blackness set into the panelling, like the secret panel in a painting of cavaliers they had in the hall at home. There came, as Barry hung back, the heavy clack of an archaic light switch and a quantity of dingy light, and then the scrape of a door opening and an upwaft of heated warm-brick air. Barry hesitated on the narrow stairs, so strait that there were no bannisters and the walls brushed his shoulders. The man below, he knew, wouldn't be the devil or anything like that, nor was it hell down there, and yet... His father called up, somewhat peevishly, and then Barry heard muffled echoing conversation and an unseen large laughter.

The side walls fell away to let the last half-dozen steps advance alone. There was an extensive expanse of gleaming floor, like a dull lake flooding the furthest corners, in pools stagnant beneath tangles of old chairs and thickets of overturned double desks piled up like the desiccated carcases of horses, and in the midst of the clear space an enormous but quite prosaic dull grey stove, the shape of a giant peppermill. Piles of steely coke stood crisply beneath the debouchures of the coke shutes.

The big man with the dirty face came out of the thicket and grunted a box over and onto a horse that was still on its feet. Ridiculously large he lowered his rump onto a tiny scholar's chair and mumbled something with a sly smile in Barry's direction. His father wore a silly boyish expression on his face, one he had never seen before, and the man laughed shortly and rubbed the back of his hand across his nose. 'Well, Jack,' said his father, being serious again, 'We'll be off. Thanks.' 'Right you are, Mr Lyons,' said Jack, grave again, and Barry was left to bring up a loose-flapped cardboard box, with loose jingling stuff sliding about in it. Jack's mime had only made it look heavy. When they arrived back in the brightly lighted hall it somehow seemed to Barry to have halved in size. His father waited by the swing doors, holding one open for him, switched off the lights and they went out to the car to take them home.

Jamaica Farewell

Sudden jangle of the phone made him jump and nearly drop what he was holding. Carefully but swiftly one hand took the weight of the dressing table's top drawer, while the other hand, also expert in this task, pushed firmly at the drawer's green bakelite knob, sliding the drawer home without it jamming or squeaking. The marbles, glaucous and pitted with age like ice-clad asteroids, rolled lazily in the complex-smelling darkness at the back of the drawer.

Downstairs the phone rang on. Then he heard the shivering crash of the glass-panelled hall door and his mother's harsh voice announced loudly: 'It's all right; I'll get it.' There was a brief interval, just as he had expected, before she picked up the receiver. She never managed to pick it up in one neat lift, but rolled it about clumsily first in its cradle.

'Hello? Luton five-oh-three-two; Mrs Dakin speaking.'

He came silently out onto the landing and perched on his haunches behind the bannisters - not the unfriendly row of hard spindles he had seen in other houses, but one honey-coloured panel which curved round and down the stairs to where his mother stood at the phone, whose station was the little shelf beside the front door. He was not watching, but listening intently. His father said that calling yourself Mrs when you answered the phone was common and only cleaning women did it. It was a title of respect and one didn't have the right to confer titles on oneself. It was as if he were to start calling himself Sir. 'Sir Dakin! Sir Dakin!' Gavin had chanted. 'Be quiet, dear; your father's talking,' said his mother quickly. With a gentle push behind Gavin's head she sent him off to wash his hands. 'He's only a little boy, darling. Don't be so angry with him. You frighten him sometimes.' His father harrumphed, and fetched his pipe. Mrs Dakin disagreed with him wholeheartedly, but silently, over this Mr and Mrs business. He was quite simply wrong. She knew that. They were like names, not titles. The butcher and so on called her Mrs Dakin - what else could they possibly call her? Titles were things that dukes and royalty had. She had said nothing, then, but carried on buttering Gavin's bread for him. Sometimes Gavin was just as pernickety as his dad: the egg had to be just right, yolk runny and white firm, or he wouldn't eat it. The way he had of plunging the first soldier into the hot yolk up to his waist and then of pulling him out, peering suspiciously to see if any of the runny albumen he hated had come up, was so like his father. Harry's face wore the same expression when the marmalade pot was inspected for the inevitable flecks of butter left by a careless knife. His toothbrush moustache would twitch petulantly and his eyes glower but never a word of reproach as he set the pot back untouched. Later his wife would pick the contamination out.

'Hello? Luton five-oh-three-two. Mrs -' It was a call-box then. 'Aowh, it's you, dear. Harold! It's Leslie. Oh, hallo, dear; I was just this moment thinking about you.'

Upstairs, on the landing, Gavin rolled about on the warm brown carpet, hugging himself with delight. He whooped and shouted without letting a sound pass his lips. He rubbed his nose right down into the dusty warm pile of the carpet, closed his eyes and doubled his legs up. Downstairs his father's voice began to boom heavily from the kitchen: 'I can't hear you, dear. I can't hear you.'

'Where are you, Leslie?' said his mother. 'Are you coming home? I'll do a nice cake for you, specially. A seed-cake. Or would you like a chocolate...oh but - Harold! He's in a phone-box on Alexandria Avenue.'

Alexandria, Alexandria, sang Gavin to himself, crawling forward to peep down the stairs. His father came into the hall with his half-limping heavy gate, fingers worrying away at the bulbous part of his nose, tugging and squeezing at it. Standing there indecisive in his red carpet slippers, he glanced up and saw Gavin, who was staring with astonishment back at the grin of delight spread across his father's normally quite harassed-looking face. With a jolt, Gavin understood his father was just as pleased as he was that Leslie was coming home, which was strange; he always thought he didn't really enjoy his son's visits. The last time Leslie came home, they had interminable wrangling discussions in the living room in the near-dark about things called Suez and Nasser and Macmillan. Macmillan was the name of Mr Dakin's boss at work; who the others were, he couldn't say. And when Leslie was there, his father never looked pleased - in fact, it was just like the times before Leslie had gone away. It was different with his mother, mothers were always pleased about things like that. Chris's mother, Mrs Lambert, had nearly gone hysterical when her Philip had come home, pushing Gavin out of the house, which smelt funny anyway, so that she could tidy up.

A jarring clunk as his mother put the receiver down. She dabbed at her eyes with the small white lace handkerchief she carried in her apron. Gavin hated it. If he had a smut on his face, she would wet the handkerchief with a little spittle and dab the horrid-smelling thing at him, who squirmed away from it.

'Will you pick him up in the car then, Harold? And I'll get myself ready.'

Making little darting grooming movements at her hair, she came up the stairs towards him, seeing him for the first time. 'Oh, Gavin, darling, Leslie's coming home. He'll be here any minute now. Dad's going to pick him up.'

Gavin made a face to show that he already knew.

'Get a clean shirt on now, Gavin, and brush your hair, there's a good boy.'

He made another face as she disappeared into her bedroom. From the rustle of clothes she called out: 'And have a good scrub-down wash, too!'

'Oh, Mum, I've already had one.'

'Well, have another, being clean never hurt nobody.'

'Aoh, Mu-um.'

It was typical how they spoilt everything.

'Gavin!' she said warningly. 'Do as you're told: I'll not have you whining and being difficult when I've got such a lot on.'

Gavin said nothing more, wise from long experience, but turned on the wash basin taps. He put in the plug and, pulling off his grey flannel shirt, wetted face and hands. Then he made splashing noises with the nail brush for a while before letting the still pure water gurgle out. 'Don't forget to clean off the rim, Gavin.' He turned the taps quickly on and off.

Back in Leslie's room, he sneaked the drawer open again. Everything seemed to be there all right: the pile of clean white handkerchiefs; the penknife with the marbled handle; the double-ended pencil with red and blue leads that met at some hidden place in the shaft; the open crimpled packet of the strong Clarnico mints that gave this drawer its characteristic smell. The middle drawer smelt strongly of French polish from the time Leslie had kept his French polishing kit here. Now it was his sports drawer: there was the puncture outfit in its long round-ended tin. Gavin knew all of its components: the variform rubber-backed patches; the wee plastic tub, closed by a pin, that held the fine chalk-dust; the flattened, curled and crinkled tube of rubber solution and the spare valves. Leslie had a Michelin map of France with a picture of Bibendum on the front, and also a couple of cycling club calendars, one pink and one blue, made of a funny, half-shiny sort of card with stuff like gauze sandwiched into it somehow. At the bottom, a dog-eared spare parts catalogue that smelled strongly of oil, but it was still no match for the lingering ghost of the departed polish. Gavin wondered if Leslie would notice that he had scrumped some of his mints. He had only taken three, since Christmas, and had only been going to keep them for the smell. But he had eaten them, one by one. Everything in place. He closed the drawer.

'You shouldn't be in there really, Gavin; Leslie wouldn't like it.'

'I was just looking at the yacht again, Mum.'

'Let me see your hands,' she said, stopping him at the door before he could sideslip past. 'You haven't washed, Gavin, you little monkey.' She tugged him into the bathroom. 'Look, the soap's still dry.'

'Leslie's here!' he shouted, hearing a car pull up outside and not caring whose it was. Immediately, his mother's fingers relaxed slightly, and Gavin twisted nimbly away. The front door bell clanged its two mellow, descending tones.

Then Gavin remembered something, something he had forgotten to put back into its home in the drawer. It was hidden now in his room, pushed in between the mattress and the springs of his bed, at the wall side just to be sure. He could lie in bed with his face pushed into the fresh linen smell of the pillow and push his arm round under the mattress until his fingers touched the relic.

She had taken her apron off and was now wearing her jungle dress - that was Gavin's name for her handsome lime-green and black frock, patterned with hands of jagged-edged narrow leaves. The green was so shrill that it was almost yellow and Gavin admired this colour very much. Standing for a moment at the top of the stairs before going down to answer the door, his mother flicked up her skirt and darted a hand below to check if her suspenders were secure. Gavin knew that there was something vaguely naughty about this and about looking, but he couldn't help it. She checked that her seams were straight and smoothed down her frock at the back, telling Gavin to behave and not get over-excited and to give Leslie some peace and quiet. The bell clanged again and she thumped down the stairs.

Two shapes flickered and bobbed, distorted by the rippleglass of the leaded lights, and then his mother, fumbling nervously at the latch, finally had the door open, to frame a tanned white-toothed sailor in blue and white.

Gavin watched a grinning Leslie disappear as he bowed into her arms, and then she stepped back to appraise him as he stood there in front of his father, who looked somehow older and shabbier than usual. Father and son exchanged conspiratorial grins. That meant that they would go up to the Windmill on Montrose Avenue after lunch, and Mum would bake the cake, singing away to herself in the kitchen. Gavin wanted a seed cake: light and airy and pale yellow with a slightly sugary crust and speckled throughout with caraway seeds.

Gavin lurked shyly on the stairs and blushed with pleasure when his brother, wearing a real sailor's uniform, threw him a cocky wink just like Tommy Steele and called out: 'There he is, Gavin the young shaver.' He would wait, he decided, until later, when the fuss had died down and Leslie was alone, and then he'd show him the fag cards, real Gallagher's, which always felt thicker in the middle than at the edges and for which he had swapped hundreds of Brooke Bond's cards. Two complete sets of 'Freshwater Fish.' Leslie, he knew, had some in his drawer; a wad of them held tightly by a red rubber band. Maybe Leslie would take the hint and give him one or two. Leslie's were of famous cricketers and in a funny cartoon style that was all angles and pastel colours. Gavin had taken them to school once to show the others, but only once: he had spent the whole time subsequent to their publication sick with anxiety that one of the big boys would snatch them from him. Ritchie, for one, had tried.

Leslie and his mother, father behind beamingly lugging for his son the two heavy naval issue cardboard suitcases - Leslie called them 'pusser's cases' - loudvoiced their way into the living room. Leslie nipped back out smartly, his concertina-creased bell bottoms flapping.

'Come on, Gavin, me lad!'

Reaching into the back seat of the car Leslie sprang a globular carrier-bag through the air and down to his side with a single manly jerk. Gavin stood on admiringly, looking his brother up and down from curly head to polished toe. The blue triple-white-striped scarf, the white lanyard, and the dark jumper tight over the hip. Leslie brought his shiny boots together with a crash of the heels and saluted Gavin who ran back indoors.

Side by side, as in a customs shed, the fat suitcases waited lids to but locks sprung ready. Leslie stood before them with a proud proprietary air.

'And now the distribution of the presents.'

'Is it a birthday, Leslie?' asked Gavin and they all laughed. Presents were for birthdays or at Christmas. 'Well, is it?' he said crossly.

Leslie squatted on his heels.

'Gavin, I'm just back from the West Indies. I've been away for a long time, so it's only right and proper that I bring somefink back for me ol' mum an' dad an' me ickle bruvver.'

Gavin wondered what the West Indies might be, when something crackly was jammed roughly onto his head, fitting him all too well. A hard corner bored into his scalp.

'Oh, do be careful, Gavin, you'll break it,' boomed his father as he snatched the hat off.

STOLEN FROM HAITI screamed the straw hat in clumsy red letters. Gavin threw it to the floor and began to cry.

'Deugh-gh,' said his father, rolling his eyes. Gavin glared at him through his tears.

'What's the matter with it, Gavin?' asked Leslie gently. 'I thought he'd like it. Don't you like it then, Gavin?'

'It's not a real present,' sobbed Gavin.

'How do you make that out, love?'

'Look.' Gavin pointed to the Stolen from Haiti legend, and then everything was all right again. Leslie laughed and ruffled his hair, and jammed the hat back on just as roughly as before. Gavin smiled through his tears. Then he remembered Leslie's thingy and danced with false hilarity out of the room.

'Where's he off to?' muttered Mr Dakin suspiciously.

'This is for you, dad. I'll take them out as they come.'

Gavin ran into his own bedroom and thrust his hand beneath the mattress and tugged the object out. What it was, he did not know. It resembled a shard of pottery or perhaps a piece of shell. It was curved and irregularly shaped but fitted well into the hand. The convex surface was an unpleasant blue colour; it had been coated with a cheap kitchen paint that dried to pits, bubbles and blisters. But it was the edges of it, and one glorious spot in particular, where a piece had chipped obliquely off one corner, that held the magic. The edges were about a quarter of an inch thick and, like the edge of a book, composed of hundreds of thin layers, but here every layer seemed to have a different colour. The angled edge of the chipped part made the layers seem thicker and showed up the variety of colour all the better. Its origins were mysterious. The convex side seemed to be a piece of sandy rock and Gavin thought that someone, Leslie even, had painstakingly and over years painted all the layers on.

He slipped it back into its home in Leslie's bottom drawer, the drawer which held the leather shaving kit, and the old Luton Rugby Football Club membership cards for 1954, 1955, and 1956, in green, red, and deep blue. There was also a stick of shaving soap, mostly covered by damp silver paper and a silver-plated cigarette lighter that did not work.

'Gavin!' His father. It must have been the floorboard. 'What are you doing up there?'

'Nothing,' Gavin called shrilly. 'I was looking at the yacht,' he explained, back in the living room. They laughed over the tea cups, Leslie looking up and giving him a wink.

'His own brother comes home after I don't know how long and he'd rather look at an old yacht,' said his father with heavy humour.

'It's not an old yacht,' he said belligerently. He didn't like the way his father became stricter with him in front of other people, especially when it was Leslie and not a stranger.

'Gavin.' A note of warning, like a growl in Mr Dakin's voice.

'He's just excited, Harry; let him be. Look, darling, look at what Leslie's brought me,' and she held a garish bolt of pink, yellow and mauve against herself. Gavin liked the mauve. He hoped Leslie had not minded him being in his room - he had not seemed annoyed.

Gavin had already read quite a number of the books in the three-tier rickety bookcase in Leslie's room, sneaking them out singly, attempting to read and understand them, and then restoring them to the exact place on the shelves he had taken them from, each book returning with his secret mark on it. The book about the monkeys and the ladies who hid jewels in their bottoms he still had in his bedroom, but the book was too hard for him and somehow its obscurity rendered the events it described all the more terrifying; however, by his own ruling, that he could only take a new book when he had finished the old one, he would have to run through the darkness of it until the very last page.

Gavin stood by the table and gazed at all the wares piled up on it, like a stall at the market. A pair of highly polished salad bowls and a fork and spoon in the same tropical wood and at least a foot long to toss the salad with (later on that day they went to join the rosewood mah-jongg set in the bureau cupboard). Leslie had also brought back a set of walnut coasters, each one fitted with a freshly-minted golden Jamaican farthing at its centre, and all of them dropping snugly into their snug-lidded felt-lined walnut drum, bottomed with green baize. A straw waste-paper basket. Some maracas from Haiti. A carving of a narrow-faced woman with protruding lips and with tight spirals of brass wire for earrings. While Leslie had been pulling the goods like white rabbits out of his cases, Mr Dakin had plunged in his hands to help and pulled out some colourful long-players with a darkie's face on the cover.

'Not for you,' said Leslie roughly and blushing. He

snatched them back and Mr Dakin looked hurt. Red-eared, Leslie shoved the records back into his suitcase. The spell was broken. Gavin watched Leslie, wondering why he was so upset, what was so special about the records.

Later his mother said: 'He was tired from the journey, lovey. It's a long way from Portsmouth.'

'He said Pompey.'

'Yes, dear; that's a special sailors' word.'

Gavin thought that he would collect sailors' words and write them down in his book.

'I'm just going up to my room,' said Leslie, tugging one of the cases off the table. Mrs Dakins's eyes flicked to the deep shine of the table top but she said nothing.

'Don't be long, dear; kettle's going on soon.'

'Your mother's baking a cake this afternoon, especially,' said Mr Dakin, to show that he understood.

'Yes,' said Leslie. 'Good.'

Leslie did not come down again until lunchtime, untempted by calls that his tea was going cold. All morning they could hear the sound of distant music.

'He must be tired from the journey,' said Mrs Dakin, preparing the Yorkshire pudding mix in the biggest porcelain bowl. Mr Dakin, sat at the kitchen table, tugged thoughtfully at his meagre dewlaps as he filled out the Sunday Express crossword, doing all of the acrosses first, made a colourless noise to indicate that he had heard and was in absent-minded agreement.

'It was nice of them to let him come home.'

'It's his right,' said Mr Dakin stoutly, penning in another answer. T-A-L-L-Y-M-A-N. 'Foreign Service Leave it's called. He gets six days - that's two for every month he was out there in the West Indies. I checked.'

'It's nice, though,' said his wife.

Gavin's father snorted silently and returned to his crossword: it's capital is Port-au-Prince (5).

'Was that the siren?'

'On a Sunday? The works are closed on a Sunday, dear,' said Mr Dakin.

'I thought I heard something, that's all.'

Under the table, unseen, Gavin was trying to slide his father's slippers off without him noticing. Damp hot winds of roast beef misted the windows as the oven was opened and Yorkshire pudding mix poured in around the glistening joint. His mother said that this was what Leslie came home for. You didn't get food like this in the navy. He wasn't getting enough to eat. He looked thinner every time he came home.

'Always was wiry,' said Mr Dakin on a point of fact. 'He's looking healthier than ever.'

'They get a lot of sun out there.'

Mr Dakin snorted silently again and removed himself and his paper from the kitchen. Gavin wondered if it was going to turn out like the last time Leslie had come home: he had been out the whole day, popped back for a hasty tea and then went straight out again to meet his friends in the pub. The evenings belonged to the girlfriend, of course. Most of the family's conversations with Leslie were held in a bad temper and the bathroom while Leslie mutely shaved. He usually came home long after Gavin's bedtime. Gavin would try to stay awake, to flit out like a diminutive ghost to say goodnight to Leslie, but most often he fell asleep. He managed it once. Leslie had been very short with him, pushing him almost roughly back into his bedroom, telling him in a hoarse angry whisper escorted by delicious fumes of beer to get back to bed.

It was not to be like that this time. At lunch, during a lull in the procedure, Leslie told them in a casual, matter of fact sort of way that he would only be staying until Tuesday, Tuesday morning. He had promised to meet a shipmate in

London; they were going to do all the shows. Gavin glanced at his mother, and saw her lip tremble and tighten. Glancing brightly at the empty dishes, she stacked them with quick jerky movements and bore them out to the kitchen.

'You might have waited, Leslie,' said his father mildly.

'Thought it would be best to say it straight off, dad. Get it out of the way. You know how mum is.'

'A day and a half isn't much for your mother. Nor for me, come to that. I haven't seen much of you either. I wanted to hear all about your adventures; you know, what you've been up to.'

Both men, eyes down, cut at their beef, pushing the sections around in the gravy. Mr Dakin's gulp as he swallowed a forkload was loud in the silence.

'I've been at sea for a solid month,' said Leslie, sulkily, after a while. His father did not reply, not at first.

'Bloody hell, Leslie. One bloody month. I was a married man during the war, not a spotty kid discovering everything for the first time, and I was away for eighteen bloody months stuck in the middle of nowhere.'

'Well, you know how it is then, dad,' said Leslie slyly. Mr Dakin stood up and stacked their two plates, and took them in frosty silence into the kitchen.

His muffled indignant tones drifted back. Leslie made a wry face, and then his eyes rested on Gavin, who was still wrestling with his beef.

'Hey!' said Leslie.

'What?'

Gavin pretended to be annoyed too, in imitation of his father.

'You fancy coming down town with me, Gav? You know, for a walk.'

'Will you keep your sailor suit one?'

'If you like,' said Leslie, nodding. Gavin nodded his agreement and began squashing his cauliflower with his fork to make it less conspicuous on his plate.

'Where?'

'Just town. Walk around and that.'

The last time he had taken Gavin out with him, they had gone up to Stockwood Park one autumn Sunday afternoon on Leslie's old maroon Vespa to the Rugby Club, where Leslie wangled a game with his old team. 'See you later, kid,' he said and trotted off to get changed. Bored with playing by himself in the cold long grass and dead leaves by the side of the pitches, Gavin disgraced himself by pulling the laces out of the spare ball he had found on the touchline. After that, he had nearly been interfered with by an old man, well known in the park. Leslie, coming over after his shower with fourpence bus money for Gavin, had driven the old man off.

They walked down Leagrave Road, Leslie whistling the new tune he had, past the closed gates of the Skefko works, under the railway bridge and round the corner into Bury Park and Dunstable Road. 'It's a nice day, innit?' said Leslie, looking jauntily about him, and acknowledging the occasional toot from a passing car. Gavin bounced along contentedly beside him, looking him up and down. Leslie called in at a sweet-shop, where he bought some Clarnico mints and some wine gums.

'It's my big brother,' Gavin explained to the old lady.

'That's our school sweetshop,' he told Leslie,' and that's Chalky's dad's shop.'

Leslie passed Gavin the gumdrops.

'Too strong for you these are, kid,' said Leslie, unwrapping a mint. 'Burn your mouth out.'

'Aohw, Leslie.'

'Remember when you tried the mustard?'

They stopped while Leslie looked into the window of a

record shop. 'Teds' music,' said Leslie disgustedly - then they walked on past the school and down the hill by the Post Office and the Town Hall. Here they were brought to a sudden halt by a brace of girls who knew Leslie appearing round the corner.

They were very pretty, but quite mad in Gavin's eyes: they grinned continually while they chattered on and shrieked with laughter whenever someone else said anything, no matter what, and ruffed Gavin's hair. He quite liked that. And Leslie couldn't stop grinning once he'd started either.

'This is your little brother then, Les?'

'He's cute.'

'Must run in the family.'

Leslie glowed.

'It's the uniform,' he explained to his uncomprehending brother once the girls had waved their way away. 'It gets them, it really does.'

On George Street, past the Town Hall, they went inside and up narrow stairs to the Harlequin where they had a funny sort of bubbly coffee that Gavin had only tried once or twice; the bubbles stuck to the side of the cup as you drank. Even the cup was funny: it was glass and very wide and shallow with a tiny handle. Mrs Dakin usually took him into the Milk Bar on Bute Street when they were in town. Leslie seemed to know a lot of people in the coffee bar, people who nodded and waved and called to him as they waited in line at the counter. Even down the counter girls greeted Leslie with special friendliness. Gavin noticed how white every face was in comparison to Leslie's with its new tan. They carried their coffees down the two or three steps into the back lounge and to a free table, everyone smiling at Gavin as he tried to keep his coffee from spilling out of the saucer. A long-haired girl in a tweed skirt came over to stroke his hair, while he tried to look as if he didn't really like it. The girl smelt nice. He asked for another coffee and Leslie gave him a shilling.

When he got back, running the gauntlet of smiles once more, there was another girl, with short blond hair and a pert nose, talking earnestly to Leslie. Gavin put his coffee down with a lurch and hoisted himself into a chair.

'When are you going back then, Les?' asked the girl.

'Tomorrer,' replied Leslie with a frown.

'Can't you stay...?'

'Like I said, I'm off tomorrow.'

'Yeah, well,' said the girl. 'It's a shame, that's all. Sandra was in earlier, too.'

Leslie didn't say anything to that but toyed with his spoon in the empty cup watching Gavin carefully sipping at his brimming cup, which tried to swing in his grasp. With another moue, reproachful this time, the girl went back to her table and eager girl-friend.

'Let's go, kiddo,' said Leslie, lighting a cigarette. Gavin had never seen him smoke before. The cigarette had a long blue stripe down its length.

'Pusser's snouts,' said Leslie and Gavin stared.

'Your hat, your hat, you've left it behind,' cried Gavin on the stairs, knowing how important every bit of the uniform was. 'I'll get it.' Back in the coffee bar, he bet the girls were still talking about it.

They went home on the bus. Leslie went straight up to his room for a 'catnap'. Gavin stood in front of the living-room fire and told his parents all about the pretty girls they had seen in town. Upstairs, Leslie's gramophone started up and Gavin recognized the melody filtering distantly through the floorboards as the tune Leslie had whistled all the way into town.

'Where are you off to, then, mister?'

'I'm just going to listen -'

'Don't bother him, Gavin.'

'I'm not; I'm just going to listen on the landing.'

...Down the way where the nights are gay
And the sun shines daily on the mountain top
I took a trip on a sailing ship
And when I reached Jamaica I made a stop
But I'm sad to say, I'm on my way
Won't be back for many a day
My heart is down my head is turning around
I had to leave a little girl in Kingston town...

Mr Lippstadt's Holiday

Head bowed, Mr Lippstadt looked down to where, far below the ribbed rubber toecaps of his plimsolls were gliding forward in strict alternation, skimming soundlessly over the pink paving of the promenade. A warm afternoon, although clouds were moving up. When you walked back in the evening, you could feel the heat that the stone had drunk up over the day seeping through your worn-down soles.

Dusk was dangerous: the air was cooler and slid in under your shirt. Refreshing but treacherous. Could even be fatal. Better to carry a cardigan out with you in the morning over one arm.

Mr Lippstadt glanced up ahead. Not making much progress. The promenade and beach stretched ahead of him, like a multicoloured band on the striping of a deckchair. The seafroth on the beach – a yellowish-grey line. Then a wide strip of dirty grey sand and the brown concrete of the sea wall. After that the broad pink swathe of the promenade before the pattern was lost in the anarchy of the railings, fences, palings and low walls of the boarding-houses. As the eye looked to the horizon, this multicoloured band narrowed, swinging in a lazy curve which disappeared at the outskirts of the next resort. Dark smudges apparently floating on the sea there were bathing huts and beach cafés. Under the distant pier the water shimmered.

The sea wall. Concave to break the smash of the waves in winter. Harsh edges to it that scraped and scratched the shins of scrambling children. Near the pier and the sandy steps down to the beach, people lay along in its concavity head to toe in long chains like goods wagons in a siding. Or they sat at its foot, with towels interposed between skin and concrete, and peeled the shells from hard-boiled eggs.

Green posts linked by double green pipes topped the wall. Skinny-bottomed teenagers sat on the top pipe with their feet hooked behind the lower one; solitary men rested their forearms there and peered down into the bosoms below. Posts and posts arched away on either side with the promenade. At every eighth post a heavy corporation bench had been deposited at some remote time by sweating council workmen. Solid iron, cast iron, I should think. And the wood, thick and reliable. Corporation fellows, in the off-season, had got as much paint on the pavement as on the benches. Funny how they all faced the wrong way. You came here to look at the sea, not at a row of pink and yellow boarding-houses that stared back at you. Designed for the stroller perhaps. More pleasant to dawdle past rows of ruddy smiling faces than to skulk past behind a lot of tops of heads and hanging jumpers and towels. If you wanted to look at the sea here, well, you could lean on the railings or go down onto the beach. People, thought Mr Lippstadt, preferred watching other people to anything else.

A funny resort, this one, though. A lot of people on their own, like me, or gathered into single-sex clusters, or middle-aged couples, worker dad and working mum. Not so many young people, but a few kidnapped grandchildren. None of these cocky young whatevers that try to buy you drinks you don't want. They must have all flown off to Spain to annoy people there.

Mr Lippstadt sat for a while on one of the corporation benches. The green paint was still glossy. They'd painted it straight over the previous coat, without stripping it first; you could still see the craters where last year's paint had blistered and popped in the sun. Mrs Taylor's lad, Steve, that's what he did one summer. Him and another lad, both students, they'd painted the railings all the way from the bottom of Crawley Road, under the bridge with the icy shadow and then as far as Wardown Park and back again on the other side. Brighter green though. But lemon and pink! You couldn't get away with painting your house with colours like that anywhere except the seaside. Bed and Breakfast. No Vacancies. TV Lounge. Straight out of the house, open the front gate and you're on the prom.

Clumps of pensioners dozed in deckchairs outside the boarding-houses. Jolly-faced women chaffed. Old George there still got an eye for the lassies. Pretty little thing that. Ho, ho, old George, chuckled the men, flirting with chubby matrons of fifty or fifty-five. No figures but still had the glad eye. Men in braces dozed with folded copies of the Daily Mirror over their faces.

Hot now. Seventy-eight or -nine. In London, the paper said, they were putting tables outside the pubs on the pavements, just like in Paris. Can't see much point in sucking in diesel fumes with your pint.

Couldn't look up now. The sun's glare bounced up off the pavement under his guard. Out of the corner of his eye he saw the ornate end-pieces of the benches, pastel-painted gate posts, puffy pale legs of deckchair occupants with balls of wool twitching at their feet. Straight out of your digs onto the prom. No cars revving up at night, or engines idling for minutes on end while the driver murmured and nuzzled his departing passenger.

At Southend once. The streets reeking of stale beer. He had stood and watched a man tumble out of a pub and then stagger off, thrashing with his arms and singing. At eleven o'clock in the morning. And he had nearly got himself run over by a young thug in a car. Baby-faced, as they say in the newspapers, with his pallid and fragile girlfriend frightened beside him. He had seen the thug's face behind the wheel and how he had wanted to kill the drunk. Had killed him if there weren't laws and policemen and gaols.

Mr Lippstadt went back to the hot dryness of north Africa. Like putting your head inside a spin drier. During the war, when they were pulling back from El Gazala, on the road. One of their lads, a boy of eighteen or so, shot a young Arab girl who had been taunting them from the doorway of a ruined house and had jeered at his threatening rifle. He hadn't known how to save his face and lower the gun.

Holidays – when you can just walk along with your hands in your pockets. These old flannels. Bought them off a chap called Simmons who played for the Hong Kong Cricket Club. Transferred by the company to Java where they didn't play cricket. Ground too mushy.

Mr Lippstadt's fingers, as every year, encountered the dust of ancient and mouldered custard creams.

Isle of Wight. He had never been here with his wife, so danger of memories. Couldn't not take a holiday though. Do me good. Sort things out in my head. Bone-achingly miserable again for the first week. Dry sobbing on his bed in the afternoons. One afternoon he took the slightly antiquated Vectis bus from Ventnor to Blackgang Chine. Walk around, tea in the tea-house with a packet of biscuits. Watching that girl over the top of the newspaper. Then she was leaving and he got up suddenly, without thinking, and hurried out after her. Snickers from some of the tables. Burnt my throat on the hot tea. Stuffed the rest of the biscuits into my pocket.

Couldn't see her anywhere at first. Then he saw a telescope on a stand, pushed in a sixpence, and quickly scanned all the rising and plunging paths of the chine. Bordered with rhododendrons and rustic latticework.

Further on, way ahead of him, the buzzing coast road, held away by the town from the shore, dived suddenly seawards to slide noisily alongside the promenade and accompany it right into the centre of Acton-on-Sea. There lamp standards dangled with multicoloured lights, which you could see at night if you leant far enough out of the bedroom window.

Maybe Acton-on-Sea would have been a better place to have gone to. Not so many old people. Couple of hours to walk there, then back in comfort on the top deck of one of those open-topped buses. They could have told me the times at the hôtel, no, boarding-house. If I'd asked.

Damn! Walked straight past without noticing. A young mother with baby. On a bench she sat, straight-backed, her slim arms raised to the pushbar of the baby-carriage, peeking and cooing at him smiling in his little sunhat. Couldn't possibly go back now, look wrong. The woman's frock shone livid white tinged with a trace of lemon, and the design resembled dark splatted purple raspberries. Like those we ate after the war in Canada. Ticonderoga. A wide warm terrace, balustraded with biscuit-coloured stone, overlooking a wide lake. Warm nights. And from the yellow wall of French windows behind them, a trumpet soloed, holding back almost intolerably before yielding to the inevitable ictus, like a man stealing instants from his ardour. They stood silently, him listening, an arm about her waist, beneath the soft white globes of the lamps. Cherry-blossom pink. Mr Lippstadt clicked the memory off, and the room was dark and empty again.

A few steps further on he permitted himself a rest, at a rare bench that faced the sea. He looked back, turning with difficulty his head upon a stiff neck, to measure his progress. An aerial landscape of mountains and ravines was advancing over the town. Still in the sun, there sat the dark-haired young mother in her raspberry dress now gazing out to sea while her baby gurgled in his pram. Much further back, in the shadow of the cloud cliffs, a blob of vivid turquoise which he knew was the Aertex shirt of the male half of a couple he had overtaken half an hour before near the pier. They were still clumping doggedly forward like a pair of uncarapaced tortoises. The man worked his jaw continuously, almost furiously. His wife held fiercely onto his arm. She wore a raincoat.

The first time he had attempted the promenade walk it had not been a success. The sky had been novembral. Folded-up newspaper in one pocket, folded-up plastic mac in the other. He planned to have fish and chips for lunch in a seafront restaurant in Acton-on-Sea, take a deckchair on the beach and doze an hour or two away in a pleasant fashion. Then heavy raindrops dropped like berries to burst on the pavement releasing the smell of rain. He took his newspaper into an evil-smelling little shelter on the promenade which was unhappily occupied. He had to squeeze between a glum and irritable family group and a brace of plump old women redolent of wet wool. The little boy whined and kicked at this shoes in front of the adults' listless gaze until roughly hauled away by one arm by his mother. Mr Lippstadt endured this compulsory entertainment, his stomach rumbling with hunger, until the rain cleared.

As if conjured up by his memories of that wet miserable Thursday, rain tumbled noisily down, spattering in large dark patches. Just the worst sort of weather for these clothes. Never learn. All night long, the people in the room next to his, the Garstons, built like a pair of Irish bullocks, had been copulating noisily. Every evening after dinner, they went off down to the pub, to return long after closing time. Lying alone in bed, Mr Lippstadt could hear through his open window Mr Garston's stream battering the rhododendron bush just around from the front door and then Mrs Garston giggling. In the night the grind of the neighbouring sash window being heaved up and a sound of pattering from the bushes below. In the dining room, Garston's taurine eye followed the lank-haired skivvy as she cleared plates from the tables, while all the time he rubbed his socked foot against his wife's thick ankle.

Men looked younger to him now, all of them. Women didn't. They seemed to exist on a separate time scale, whereby you evaluated their age and attractiveness absolutely, without reference to your own. Whereas the oldest man in the boarding-house, a solitary round man in his late seventies, to his mind resembled a sad schoolboy, despite his baldness and the great hanging empty bags under his eyes. No, that had not been quite true: not all women. The unattractive did not exist to him. Never had.

Tuesday evening he had longwhiled away in the residents' lounge. As if anyone else would want to come in there. Outside the rain plapped down onto the slimy concrete of the backyard. That's Mr Leighton's seat; he's coming back, squawked one of the crones at him, catching him shifting the wad of creased newspaper, now rather greasy to the touch, onto another less desirable chair. He's coming back, echoed the other. Tinny tintinnabulations of a tiny bell. Mrs Welling's budgerigar jerked stiffly from perch to perch in its jangling cage. The crones had the privilege of feeding the bird with fragments of biscuit soaked in tea. The residents peered with absurd concentration at a programme on commercial television during the course of which the Garstons thudded their way into the room and creakingly occupied the sofa. From time to time Mr Lippstadt glanced up from his book. Mr Garston's hair was slicked back with a substance that smelt of motor oil and which probably left marks like newsprint smudges on the antimacassars.

Closing his small red Cruikshank-illustrated copy of A Christmas Carol in the midst of his eleventh or twelfth voyage through it, he slowly ascended the back stairs to his room. Guests are respectfully requested not to shave in the bathrooms. What you were supposed to do, Mr Lippstadt had learnt after enquiry, was to fill a pitcher with hot water from the bathroom geyser which Mr B Welling would operate for a charge of 2d. This was also the charge for a bath, which certainly required more water than a shave. The shaving could be performed in your shadowy bedroom, with the bowl set on the dresser, and by peering bent almost double into the murky bespeckled mirror which kept tipping forward until Mr Lippstadt learnt to jam his bottle of hair tonic under its lower edge and thus assured its inclination.

The rain shower petered out in a series of distinct patters on the thin tin of the shelter, this time empty. This time Mr Lippstadt need not suffer hunger: in his pockets he had sandwiches. He had come across a little place on the sea-front, a café of sorts, which seemed, to judge from its outside, to be either a barbershop or else an American ice-cream parlour. Inside, he drank hot sweet tea and mumbled his way through a packet of soft biscuits. Over a second cup he chatted to the unshaven proprietor. He ordered two rounds of cheese sandwiches, to be picked up after nine o'clock, nine hundred hours, said the man, putting out a feeler, the next morning. His third cup of tea was on the house. He would eat the sandwiches when he got to the end of town.

Voices from the sea. From his elevated position on the promenade he looked down onto the beach. With nostalgia his eyes traversed two lovely anatomies in bikinis, with cardigans and beach bags by their heads. The flat stomachs bracketed by the twin knolls of the pelvis. One of them perhaps sensed his eyes, although innocent, palpating her and swung herself abruptly up on one sharp elbow to glare coldly at him. Mr Lippstadt reddened with anger. Making me feel like a Peeping Tom. Faces never matched up. Looking at her in exactly the same way as one would a statue of Venus in the museum.

Bloody ridiculous climate England has. When we were out in Canada, staying out at Teddy's place, Ste Hyacinthe, you could walk out in the morning in your shirt sleeves and not think about the weather. Autumn was autumn, too. Mont St Bruno in the fall. From the road you could see, Don slowed the convertible, a white cross high up on the steep mountainsides where a boy scout falling from the peak had hit the ground. Acres and acres of fruit orchard roofed the lower slopes. Couldn't see the ground for waxy red apples. Like a shingle beach in red. Or thousands of necklaces which had burst their strings.

The sky loured. Slack canvas stripes of vacated deckchairs wobbled in the concreted front gardens of the boarding-houses. Inside, in dank lounges, men got up fours for rummy. A small rain began to fall. The next shelter was the bus stop, where the coast road achieved its union with the promenade. Here to stay. He could feel the cold mist on his face. Loitering in one of the doorways was out of the question. In the distance, out at sea over an indistinct sealine, the purple sky belched and Mr Lippstadt felt the onset of a colder, steelier rain, driving in between his shoulder-blades and pinning his damp shirt to his back. Bloody silly, if not suicidal, leaving the mac behind. He hated the way plastic macs channelled cold rain down inside sleeve and collar while the edge of the plastic chafed the skin raw.

The long line of watermelon-pink, lime-green and lemon-yellow boarding-houses came to an end at a vast triangular area of rubble-strewn concrete the colour of old dishcloths, across which, on its far side, standing sturdily behind a blue fence of corrugated iron plastered with circus posters, he saw a dumpy round tower. Approaching across the windy concrete, clammy flannels sticking to thigh and shin, Mr Lippstadt recognized the source of the mysterious 200 which could be seen from his room, hanging far off in the resort's night sky. A rusty iron frame carrying rows of milky light bulbs was fixed near the top of the tower. Not 200, he saw, but ZOO. The circus posters here and in the town were not advertising a circus but the zoo here. A gap in the corrugated iron, two posts supporting a gimcrack construction of cracked dirty-white lathes meant entrance and, to him, shelter.

Simba, Star of TV and Hollywood. With his Trainer, ex-TV Tarzan, Mr Lloyd Pharr. Visit the Monkey House. See the amazing Snake Man wrestle the giant Anaconda. Morning Performances. Children's matinees.

He stood for a moment before the entrance, wondering whether the zoo were closed or not. Scuffed-up lolly wrappers caught like dead leaves at the base of the wire mesh fences or piled up in corners. A chained-up Walls fridge, pale blue and dirty yellow, spattered with wobbling raindrops, stood outside on the concrete. And there was someone in the ticket booth, behind the glass, after all. An old man with bulging blind eyes, head sunk within a jacket much too large for him. Yer can get coffee in the caffyteria, he said, pushing the curl of ticket across. It's raining, said Mr Lippstadt. I forgot to bring... 'S normal, said the old man, moving his head as if he were looking him up and down with his ear. Ain't nuffing special. 'S not bleeding Siam, is it? Well, said Mr Lippstadt, as a matter of fact, that... But he could tell the man was not listening.

The doorway, coming almost immediately after the wet turnstile, was set into the side of the tower itself. Mr Lippstadt assumed that the zoo, with its paddocks and so on – he knew Whipsnade – extended somewhere behind the tower. The doorway was wide and low and ogival. Steps took him down into clammy near-darkness with air that smelt as cold and dead as crypt air. Mr Lippstadt, afraid of stumbling, waited for the chamber's outlines to reassemble themselves now that they had a visitor. Catch pneumonia if I hang around in here. Arches, stone beams, trickles of brick dust, mysterious small gratings high up in the walls, and low-powered light bulbs. A blotchy, irregular line of luminous paint guided a visitor like a slug's trail through the vault.

She hadn't been able to stand darkness indoors or going underground or into cellars or things like that. A rockery had been planted where the corner house had been demolished, built on its rubble. Every family in the street bombed out and sitting on their suitcases, numb in a chill false dawn, waiting for the bus to pick them up. She had had to wait three hours in the cellar, crouched with Geoffrey under the dining-room table they had dragged down there, until the stairs had been cleared. Geoffrey's arms were a mass of bruises, she'd been gripping him so tight. The same week, Mrs Webb, who lived next door, went to post off a letter to her Jack, a stoker in the navy, and came home to find a telegram on the mat: he had gone down with the Hood.

Her letter to him about it all and he had been out on a 48-hour pass when he received it. His one and only lapse. A present to himself, really, considering everything. She'd understand. Nevertheless he had still thrown out the crying brown girl, and gone straight back to his unit before his time was up and on the same day struck a corporal.

There was another chamber, also gloomy. A flat glass case of considerable dimensions rested on a stand in the centre of the floor. It seemed, at first sight, to have been filled with cotton wool and a whispering, rustling noise came from it. Closer, there was the odour of dry decay, as of owl droppings in an abandoned barn. And another smell, like the Egyptian room at the British Museum. Methanol, formaldehyde, formalin, whatever it was. He looked down into the case. Balls of cotton wool, like children's clouds, twitched and jerked. Then he realized that the brown specks on the clouds were mouse droppings and that there were hundreds of white mice in there, redcurrant-eyed and ham-eared, nosing feverishly over, around and under each other and the clouds of cotton wool in ceaseless small rushes of activity. Or, in the corners and along the angle with the glass walls, mice lay asleep, heaped up like sacks of grain. There were no air-holes in the case as far as he could tell, nor any hatches for delivering food. He walked slowly around the case, looking for a card which would establish it as a bona fide exhibit. Disgusting. What children might think! Water in the trays (old pipe tobacco tins) all bemerded and stale.

Crypts must be like this, except that there the mice would be working away undisturbed in the darkness, inside the wood.

The brightness made his eyes blink as he came up. Patch of blue in the sky you could make a shirt from. That meant good weather. Strange place, this. The courtyard he came into was enclosed by two walls of stables (to judge by the half-doors), by the tower and by a line of shrubs, beyond which Mr Lippstadt imagined the zoo proper would commence. Paving stones had been let into the mud to form rough paths. Like a decaying riding school. Voices and laughter from two children playing behind one of the sorry trees in the centre of the compound. Black grid of a tall, narrow cage like something used for punishing heretics. As he walked towards it, he caught a whiff of something nasty, not merely the smell of rain-sodden earth. Why doesn't he jump an' that, eh, mister? said the little boy, holding his sister's hand. The monkey, its face the colour of a fig, met Mr Lippstadt's gaze for a hopeless moment. He felt that the creature would understand his words, and so, looking at the matted hair of its body, he said nothing. Look, he's got spots. All over his legs. They hadn't even given the monkey a decent perch, just a slippery pole leant against the corner of the cage. He had to keep his little black fingers hooked through the mesh to stop himself sliding down into the lake of rainwater, in which excreta and rotted fruit floated, in the bottom of the cage. The little boy had been teasing him by poking a twig at his fingers. Silly old monkey, silly old monkey, cried the children, skipping away. Mr Lippstadt and the monkey exchanged another long look.

He'd pushed her down, more out of desperation than ardour. Look, he said, holding her tightly by the wrist. Look. She made no attempt to escape or even to stand up, but sat sideways to him on the grass with her knees drawn up a little and looked up at him. And he'd stood frozen in the ridiculous posture of someone starting to go down on his knees, not knowing what to do next. I'm sorry. It's my wife. The woman, still imprisoned in his grasp, watched him. Letting go of her, he went down on his haunches and then dropped onto his knees. The ground was damp. It's my wife. Face in hands. She... He waited for the sympathetic hand. Then the woman was up on her feet and walking off, not too briskly, down the path to the chine, and all the time she had not uttered a single word or sound, had not shown a trace of emotion.

The whore in Genova, Genoa. Arranged to meet some people in a bar near the waterfront. Aragna verde, something like that. They walked the whole slow-curving length of the Via Pre, past all the whores standing like sentries and their pimps milling around in front of the toffee-apple stands and contraband cigarette vendors. Must be here somewhere. Hang on here a tick, said Captain Lippstadt, walking over, show the ditherers, to one of the line of women leaning tiredly against the shutters of a derelict shop. Scusi, signora. Dov'è l'aragna verde? Che? said the woman, not too bad really, close up, considering. He had repeated himself, wondering if somehow he had got Spanish mixed up with his Italian. The whore frowned to mirror his concentration and smiled encouragingly. Bar, l'arachnida, oh God, l'aragna. She nodded. She had understood. Letting her back slide a little way down the pillar behind her, she parted her knees. Qua, she said, and he did not look down. He blushed and tried again. Qua. Qua. And she was right. He didn't really care about the bar and those other people. There was only ever one question and one answer. Qua. Qua.

It was after Sally that all his funny ideas started. Insults to her memory, really. Prayers to her in a backstreet Methodist church with pale wooden pews, smart blue hassocks and the smell and slide of floor polish. Not that he had idealized her. The truth came to him one night as he was walking home from the local. The solitary male is a pervert. Had to be. A man on his own is an unnatural thing, so it was only logical that his desires should bend towards the unnatural. Lippstadt's Law. After retirement it wouldn't matter anymore, nothing to lose. The first time, slipping a curved palm skimmingly over the globe of a woman's buttock on the underground. Had to sit down. No one realized that it was me. Thought I was having a turn it was so strong.

Purple raspberries moved through the leaves of the shrubs.

Mr Lippstadt, nipping round them, bumped straight into the massive head of a lion on the loose, to fall with a little cry at its feet. Simba, Star of TV and of Hollywood, strained against her chain to nose at... Mister, mister, shrilled the children, until the paunchy trainer, Mr Pharr, clad in khaki shirt and jodhpurs of specially sturdy twill, came angrily out of his little hut and dropped his newspaper. Simba nudged Mr Lippstadt's arm with her nose to wake him.

The Sands of the Sea

He found it, or perhaps it found him, one Saturday afternoon spent rootling in a bookshop in Liverpool, one he had not come across before, behind Lime Street station. The signboard said, in elegant letters of old gold on royal blue, W D Troon, Bookseller and Dealer in Antiquarian Books. He did not waste a glance on the displays of new books on the ground floor, but followed the tempting arrow up the stairs to two floors and an attic crammed with second, third, and probably twentieth-hand books. Ferdy thought he would spend half an hour at the very most in there; it did not seem right passing a sunny spring afternoon in the dusty garrets of a bookshop.

Browsing commenced in the first room left on the first floor. Mr Troon did not seem to order his stock very systematically: a book on Devil's Island, next to one on travels in ancient Egypt, and then a screenplay of Nosferatu. That meant longer, as he could not skip sections. From time to time he was vaguely aware of the dull tonk of the shop's doorbell, an archaic one, quivering on a spiral spring. Ferdy's fingertips skimmed the spines of the books before him, as if he could size up the contents by palpation rather than by reading the titles. After a while he straightened up, crossed to the window and peeped out through its grimy panes to see with some relief that the sky was now overcast, and its bruised colour threatened a storm. With a lighter conscience he returned to the books.

Already a little pile of captives had accumulated, mostly paperbacks, hopping its way after him on his slow progress through the rooms, jumping from shelf to shelf, resting for a moment on table corners, or perching atop tottering stacks which crawled up the walls like petrified and broken concertinas.

He had now reached the attic stairs and it was, he felt, almost time to go. This he knew from the mounting sensation of nausea that second-hand bookshops produced in him and which the pleasures of fossicking could not for ever hold off. It was very strange, though, this queasiness. Like the creeping onset of seasickness, almost. He hastened up to the little windowless attic room and a final completion of his rounds.

This last chamber, cramped and airless, would scarcely hold anything of interest. Here the bookseller had dumped the most wretched volumes. It was a kind of charnel house. The very sorriest of the books came to rest on no shelf nor stack, but were simply tossed onto a heap in the corner as Mr Troon, he supposed, sorted through the cardboard boxes of new acquisitions on the battered deal table in the centre of the room, beneath the bare light bulb. Ferdy, in unconscious imitation, spread his catch out here to evaluate it, totting up the prices, and trying to make his mind up which ones he would take home with him.

Heavy footsteps on the stairs. Ferdy stopped what he was doing and listened. The invisible person stopped, evidently distracted by the books piled on each tread. There was a dry cough, and the stairs creaked as the browser shifted his weight more comfortably perhaps. Ferdy bent his head back to his prey. Ritual in the Dark, and The Mind Parasites, both by Colin Wilson, a new enthusiasm. The Ka of Gifford Hilary, to add to his Wheatleys. Regretfully, he cast out the 1938 Brockhaus, hiding it for a later occasion in the bottom shelf of an old book cabinet − the sort where each shelf is protected by a long glass-fronted flap. The cabinet was worth a great deal more than its contents. A greasy label still adhered by one corner to the top of the cabinet, whispering 'Magic and the Occult' in faded Victorian copperplate, although the case now held only old school history books, obsolete and unwanted. Ferdy's fingers, dropping the thick Brockhaus over the top of the bottom shelf of books into the secret space at the back, encountered another volume secreted there. It almost nudged and nuzzled at his fingers, like a cat's nose, and he drew it forth. It was a slim black volume, bound in dull black leather and even with some good tooling around the margins of the boards. The leather was scuffed and at the broken corners degraded into a dusty red substance.

Casually he flicked it open, noted the price, three pounds, which was more than he could afford anyway, but all the same the little book displayed its curious pages to him. At first glance he dismissed it as a bound collection of old almanacs, the old wives kind, so eccentric was the typography and layout, full of strange lists as well and intricately numbered matrices of words. The man on the stairs coughed again, and mounted more decisively towards the attic. On impulse, Ferdy took the little book, and pushed it into the waistband of his trousers at the back where it would be safely concealed by the hang of his jacket. Taking up his purchases he brushed past the tall thin man, the cougher he supposed, just entering the room. The man, an old man, emitted an odour of camphor, or mothballs, or some such chemical half-familiar from the biology lab at school.

On the bus Ferdy transferred the little book to an inside pocket, reflecting that this was the first time he had ever stolen anything since he had known better, but really he only intended to borrow it. He would slip it back when he had read it. Although intensely curious, for some reason he did not feel he should start reading it on the bus, so instead he gazed out of the window at the decay of Liverpool drifting past. Boarded-up houses, empty black windows with no glass, sometimes a glimpse of barred rafters against the sky where a roof had fallen in. The bus paused at a stop and idly Ferdy watched a thin old man in a dusty black coat hurry past and then disappear abruptly into the doorway of an undertaker's, one of a long line of derelict shops, boarded-up and plastered with day-glo posters: Sunday, Indo-Jazz Fusions, in Concert, Canned Heat, Black Sabbath, Civic Hall Friday 7 pm.

In the warmth and brightness of the kitchen (outside, dusk) he made himself a cup of coffee, wolfed down a hunk of his mother's parkin, and browsed through each book, leaving the little black one until last. This time he discovered, inside the back cover, a hinged pocket, which was unfortunately empty. What should have been there, he thought, a map or diagram, was sure to have been something indispensable to the book and an understanding of it. It certainly meant that the book was not worth the three pounds demanded. Possibly, it was even worthless. In time, Ferdy realized the direction this reasoning was tugging him in, and tried to accept the fact that for all intents and purposes he had stolen the book, even if he was going to unsteal it later.

He searched rapidly through the pages to see if any map or plan was mentioned there, but soon forgot his first intention, drawn in as he was by the musty scent of mystery that the words and phrases his eyes chanced to fall on gave off. Like half-formed thoughts, pictures, faint and flickering, of sphinxes, obelisks, pyramids surmounted by radiant eyes, of engravings of camels motionlessly traversing endless shimmering sandscapes, all these seemed obscurely cast upon a wall of his mind's eye by an invisible magic lantern. Ignoring a faint but persistent feeling that he should leave the book for the privacy of his nocturnal bedroom, he was soon immersed in its pages.

At first sight there seemed to be nine Lessons (unnumbered by author and printer, but pencilled in by a previous owner in careful Arabic numerals) and they bore titles, such as: a Mnemonic System; the Art of Instantaneous Recall; Cogitative Synthesis; the Three Immutable Laws; Mental Analysis and the Solution of Riddles and Conundra; the Art of Never Forgetting; Memory and Immortality. "Mine is the only true method," Professor Algol, 'formerly of Capua', claimed, "of strengthening a naturally feeble memory and a sluggish intellect. Secret vices are washed away..."

The Professor had sprinkled his product with a bizarre mixture of exhortations, reminiscent in some of a minor prophet, in others of a petty-minded and harassed clerk. "The Student should recite these words each morning upon rising, and thrice thereafter, at any convenient time. He may do so in the presence of the uninitiated, but, on no account, is he to shew these words to any third party, nor to even hint at where he obtained them." More: "He should beware of impostors claiming to be employed by the Algolic Academy. I deal directly with my pupils. I come to them. I need no intermediaries." Further on: "The Student is to supply me with his own Mnemonic Series in proof of his comprehension of the Three Laws, but he must not attempt to install any of his own creations permanently in his memory, at the risk of much damage, until my course has been completed, and he is in receipt of my 'Algolic Diploma'." From the first Lesson: "In accordance with my Principle of Secrecy, the Pupil should not attempt to communicate by a post card, which any curious eye may peruse, but by means of a sealed envelope, enclosing, should an answer be required, a stamped directed envelope. I recommend the use of a Post Office Box."

Among the lists (Xerxes 4700, Tomb 13, Cha-cha-cha 666, and so on) there were strange prohibitions: "The following Note should only be read by students well-versed in Mental Science" and "What follows will prove extremely dangerous to those Pupils who have not achieved a thorough mastery of the Sphinx-Series. These should not proceed further until the deficiency has been remedied." There was a list called the n-Series, but for what purpose Ferdy could not even guess: crown, ensign, characters, name, burden, stirrup, udder, seed, the Gambia, tribe, time, flames. Certain injunctions he found puzzling, but strangely compelling. "Let the Pupil endeavour to give special attention to this exercise, working with a metronome set at precisely 80 beats to the minute, to which frequency he should strictly and at all times adhere." The Professor also stressed that a "reliable chronometer should be purchased to enable the accurate commencement of a Recitation."

There were attacks on others: "The method of Aim, Paris, and his pupil Garaud, much aped by Mnemonical Teachers, and equally as often claimed as their own, involves the toil of imprisoning in the Memory, in a way which can only result in permanent damage to this organ, meaningless collocations of absurd dream-pictures, which of right should only enjoy a fleeting and transitory existence, being as they are the monstrous products of self-induced nightmares." Or: "Prof. Black's so-called 'peg' system; a snare for the credulous, and whereby the Knight's Tour can only be learnt successfully by committing to memory a meaningless sequence of letters, no less than 125 of them in all, a task which would perhaps take months of labour to complete, and far from being a vindication of his 'Natural System', only serves as proof of its innate absurdity."

That was enough. Ferdy was choking on the dust given off by these resurrected mummies belabouring one another with cudgels, their bandages crumbling. The book could go back next weekend. A last look, and a section written by Professor Algol to tempt scholars of foreign languages caught his eye. There was even something called a Latin Collation. Another look later. Maybe the Professor could save him the weekly detention, whenever he failed the Latin vocab test, and Mr Morris wouldn't be able to sneer. Hasta, aequor, marutina, Hermes... On his way up to his bedroom he saw the family saloon approaching down the road, it flashed its lights as it recognized him in the window, and with a show of sulky clumsiness Ferdy went out and opened the gates and then the garage doors to admit the monster with his parents imprisoned inside it and smiling at him. Ferdy gazed at them, nodded for no reason, and darted back into the house, up the stairs and into his bedroom, where he shut the door.

II

'Bring it here, boy.' Mr Morris's spectacles were two white discs. 'Yes, you, Fox,' he said in a weary monotone meant to convey an amused tolerance of the boys' little tricks. Knowing it was useless to argue, Ferdy got up an put the book on Mr Morris's desk. The master nodded for Ferdy to resume his seat. Ferdy, not moving, said: 'Can I have it back now, sir? I'll put it away.' The class sniggered. Mr Morris picked the book up fastidiously, glanced at the title-page. He looked up sharply at Ferdy. 'Well, well, Fox; well, well. Training our memory, is it? About time you did something for it I must say – we're all getting rather tired of seeing your face in detention.' 'That's what I think, sir,' Ferdy said hopefully, but drawing merely an ironic glance from Mr Morris. Behind him he heard Banfield's sneering hiss: 'Creepy little toe-rag.' 'Listen to this, boys,' said Mr Morris, rising. 'In this strange little book of Fox's here it says that "a certain Mr W Stanley Jevons" who allegedly has had "extensive experience as Examiner and Teacher", this Mr Jevons is of the opinion that "parents and public" – which I suppose could be stretched to include you lot – "have little idea how close a resemblance there is between teaching and writing on the Sands of the Sea."' Mr Morris paused theatrically, looked them over meaningfully, and then meditatively repeated with an undertone of satisfaction: 'Writing on the Sands of the Sea. Yes. Yes, indeed. Exactly.' Then, taking off his spectacles, he said: 'I think I'll keep this little tome for a while, Fox.'

Ferdy's unthinking wail of protest sounded such a clear note of real distress that Mr Morris was taken aback. The class turned to stare at Ferdy, in surprise or contempt, and he himself, shocked by the force of the outburst, reddened and did not know where to look. Mr Morris put his spectacles back on and in an unusually kind tone said that he should have the book back at the end of the lesson. 'Cry-baby,' Wilson behind him leant forward to murmur into his ear. Mr Morris gave them an unseen to get on with, obviously to allow him to peruse the book. More angry glances from the form, directed mostly at Ferdy. Groaning and fidgeting, the class opened books and took up pens.

Ferdy sat motionless, staring hard at the Latin master, staring at the balding patch on his crown until the latter sensed Ferdy's eyes on him, and looked up with the expression of a big cat disturbed at its prey. Ferdy looked back defiantly. And then Mr Morris's rather slippery smile seemed to suggest that he saw something novel in the situation, or in the boy, Fox. The clash of eyeballs had taken place, was still taking place, unnoticed by the class (heads down, writing). It was as if he and Mr Morris were alone, fighting perhaps, in some elevated place, and he was on the verge of winning. His mind filled with an intensely detailed picture, of Christ in the wilderness surveying the plains far below. Abruptly, Mr Morris clapped the book to, and, scratching distractedly the back of his neck, fell to staring out of the window. Then he rose, resumed his habitual expression of sneering boredom, and began pacing up and down the aisles between the desks, jabbing his filbert nail now and then into a boy's sloppy work, and giving off an aroma of masculine toiletries as he passed by, his black gown billowing.

The book plopped down on Ferdy's half-finished unseen. 'I'll do a deal with you, Fox,' Mr Morris said quietly with a studied casualness. Ferdy's eyes rested on the knuckles, whitening, of the hand which grasped the side of his desk as the master bent over him. He really must chuck the eau de Cologne on, thought Ferdy. 'Sir?' 'I'll let you off all tests – well, detentions – for a month, and then I'll test you on all the vocab as far as Lesson Twenty, and if you fail, you'll forfeit the book.' 'What does Fox get out of it, sir?' said Melthorne, Ferdy's neighbour, in his piping voice. 'Get on with your work, Melthorne, I'm not talking to you.' The question remained though, thought Ferdy. Displeased, Mr Morris said: 'Well, Fox, what do you want if you win?' Ferdy saw from Mr Morris's eyes as he waited for an answer that he really wanted the book, and that he, Ferdy, could name just about anything he desired. 'I'll take three pounds, sir. And the book, of course; but only if I get every single word right. If not, you get the book.' That seemed to show enough faith in Professor Algol, thought Ferdy. There was no mistaking the triumph in Mr Morris's eyes as he rose. 'All right, get on with your work,' he told the class, who had for a moment been impressed by Ferdy's obstinacy, only to see their original expectations confirmed by Ferdy's collapse as they saw it, settling for a measly three quid that he had put himself out of the running for anyway. Twit. 'I can't make money out of it; it wouldn't be right,' Ferdy whispered to Melthorne, who shrugged with indifference, evidently now also sharing the common opinion of Ferdy.

'Lot of fuss over nothing,' said Melthorne, curling his lip, although, Ferdy was pleased to see, he did not object to sitting beside him as usual on the bus home. 'Can't think why old Morris got so worked up, nor you either.' Melthorne took a glossy magazine out of his briefcase and, ignoring Ferdy, began to read. 16K memory, read Ferdy aslant. New US breakthrough in logic boards. Why use a machine, he thought, if you could do it yourself. Melthorne looked up. 'D'you see that film War Games? You should. It's brilliant. There's a bit where this kid uses his home computer to get air tickets for nothing. He somehow plugs into the phone network and the computer calls up every number, stopping whenever it recognizes another computer.' 'How's it do that?' 'I don't know exactly, but apparently there's some sort of answering tone it recognizes. You know, computer calls unto computer across the vasty deep. Anyway,' he said, impatient to get on with the story, 'by accident it hooks into the American nuclear defence system – and there's another good bit at the end where the big computer's gone mad and is running through all the numbers trying to find the launching codes for the missiles – like an enormous one-armed bandit – and you see all the numbers spinning, and then every time it gets one, it locks on that number and carries on trying for the rest -' 'Why?' 'Christ, Fox, I just told you: when it finally gets the whole number right, then it's Global Thermo-Nuclear War, the end of the world. I can't explain it exactly, you'll have to see it yourself.'

A week passed, in which time Ferdy had read, re-read, and read again the first half of the first lesson (itself only twenty pages or so) and had off by heart the first sixty words of the century which constituted the first sequence. Balcony, rabbit, habit, monk, blackfriar, pan, pandemonium, devil, kidney, Sir Philip Sidney, Arcadia, death, tomb, room, roam, wandering Jew - at which point the fantastic sequence of mental slides, in both senses, broke off of a sudden, as if a bulb had popped in the magic lantern. What came after 'wandering Jew'? What was the link? He fended off the temptation to peek at the book. Must do it from memory. Knew it yesterday. What was the logical connection? Professor Algol had forbidden picture-making, but helplessly he watched forming in his mind's eye the unbidden image of a scrawny man in sodden raiment climbing to the tossing quarterdeck of a foundering galleon. Flying Dutchman? No, that wasn't it. The Jew-Dutchman's eyes fixed despairingly upon Ferdy's before the power cut again. Then Ferdy was back in his room again, with its well-lighted dry warmth, the plastic Black Knight of Nuremberg standing stiffly upon his little plinth, the bed and the bookcase, the muted wrangling of the people inside the television set in the room below him. He opened the book again, reading ahead, coming upon another diagram. Closer inspection revealed that it was part of a savage attack on the system of yet another of Professor Algol's rivals. What is the next word? screamed the Dutchman from his page.

Ferdy, tired from a night of vivid dreams, nevertheless called in at the library on the way home from school to see if they had anything by the Professor. Mr Aster, the librarian, was determined to be helpful. He was a gawky man, in his late twenties perhaps, with an unpleasant grating voice, and was the only male amongst all the girls and married women who worked there. Ferdy did not feel entirely at ease with Mr Aster, who stood quite close and gently exuded wafts of rosewater. 'Nothing here,' he said finally, heaving shut an enormously fat red book whose pages kissed with a moist thud. 'I'll get onto it myself. Come in on Monday and I'll see what I have for you.' 'No, really -' Ferdy protested, embarrassed. 'No, no, no,' said the librarian, fluttering his hands,' It's no trouble at all.' He became confidential. 'You've no idea how I love a bit of detective work like this. Otherwise it's all old ladies and what should they read - you know.'

So he had to go back. Mr Aster took him to one side, and told him that he had gone as high as the British Library - telephonically, of course, he whinnied - and apparently they had had a copy of a book by Professor Algol, no title, but entered at Stationers' Hall [1892] but they had been unable to find their copy. 'Probably stolen,' said Mr Aster, with a prim moue of disapproval. 'You've no idea how many books we get stolen. With some of them it's almost as if there's a conspiracy. D'you know, for example, that

Walter Hannah's exposure of freemasonry is systematically stolen from every library in the country?' Ferdy said he didn't.

Wary of further conversation with Mr Aster, he left as soon as was polite. The librarian had given him a square of paper: 'Prof. Algol [pseud.] Member of the Golden Dawn. Pub. "Unsterblichkeit und der Vampirismus" Munich 1910. Died 1923 (?)'

By then Ferdy had mastered the sequence, all hundred words of it, incantating forwards and backwards as prescribed, along the self-same tortuous path of verbal stepping-stones, blindly trusting that there was a purpose in it all, that it would eventually lead somewhere and was not a meaningless jig in the dark. The desiccated voice of Professor Algol, preserved for him in the little book, commanded that the next task of the novice be to recite the whole sequence before an impartial Umpire.

It was, of course, Melthorne that obliged, amidst the clamour of the school bus. 'Lot of cock,' he said contemptuously once Ferdy had triumphantly regained the first word, having been to 'eternity' and back. 'Can't see how it's going to help you pass the test. You might as well give it to Morris. This what that book says you've got to do?' Ferdy nodded, which he reasoned did not violate the Professor's prohibition about speaking about the book. He took back the paper, which Melthorne was about to crumple up and toss on the floor, folded it carefully, and tucked it into his breast pocket.

'Think you'll manage the test?' Melthorne asked roughly, hiding, Ferdy saw, friendly concern. 'You must be sweating; it's not far off now.' Ferdy shrugged.

'I don't know,' he said. 'I've got to learn the technique the proper way, otherwise it won't work at all, and the Latin stuff doesn't come for ages yet.'

Melthorne snorted with a superior air. 'I wouldn't bother if I were you. Save your energy, nobody needs a memory these days - just bung it all in your computer's. That way it's your slave and not the other way round. All these school teachers are years behind the times.'

Ferdy shifted uncomfortably in his seat, knowing Melthorne was right. Melthorne smiled.

'Look,' he said. 'Why don't you come round my place one day after school, and you can have a go on my computer.' Ferdy nodded. 'After the test,' he said.

That night work on the Second Sequence commenced, playfully entitled the Cradle-Grave Sequence, since these words marked the beginning and end of the sequence. Now Ferdy discovered a strange thing – or was it the other way about? – that whereas the words of the first sequence had been for the most part flat, slightly colourless images, virtual abstractions, pale phantoms shackled together by the mental chains of Algol's devising into a kind of logical chain gang, the words of the second sequence, on the other hand, had a three-dimensionality to them. In his mouth they tasted solid and round, like boiled sweets or strange resinous lumps, cold pebbles, polished glass marbles, raspy rounds of pumice stone, and their nature seemed to him to be totally unconnected with their sound or significance. He wondered whether this was another side-effect of memory training, or rather a further evidence of his illicit picture-making.

Two or three times a day, then, he tongued his way along this rosary, and each time the rosary grew by a few more beads. At school, Mr Morris rarely let a lesson pass without some reference, direct or indirect, to the approaching test, and his eyes glittered to see Ferdy's diminishing confidence. Ferdy was feeling more and more acutely the impossibility of reaching the Sixth Lesson within a week. So he would lose the book then.

It was getting difficult to sleep. When he finally climbed into bed, his brain teemed away, and hours later, when he had at last fallen asleep, he would awake suddenly, hours before dawn, from dreams more real and more compelling than ever before, as stark as childhood nightmares. Themes and characters from the sequence queued up to fight their way into his dreams, where he was no passive spectator, but a struggling part of their craziness. The only conclusion Ferdy could come to was that he was violating some unknown instruction of the Professor's - perhaps the prohibition on picture-making – but there was no way he knew of stopping a thought when it was already thought, nor, he found, of turning back on the course he had set himself.

'Sorry, Fox,' Mr Morris said, hardly bothering to hide his smugness. 'Sixty-six out of ninety – nowhere near good enough.' Ferdy did not bother to dispute the figures: he had known beforehand he would fail. There had been no point learning the words until he had reached Lesson Six in the little book. 'In fact,' said the master, savouring the moment, 'You actually did percentagewise worse than you usually do. I don't think that book of yours has been a lot of help, has it?'

'I haven't finished it yet, sir,' said Ferdy in a neutral tone.

'Evidently.'

The class waited expectantly for the surrender; strangely enough, Ferdy sat quietly, apparently indifferent to the rising tension. Mr Morris decided to face him out, knowing him to be a weak, easily-led sort of boy. He waited up on the dais, chin jutting, eyes raised in ironic fashion to the ceiling, hands clasped behind his black gown.

'You do recall our little bargain, Fox?'

'Yes, sir. I lost, so you win the book.'

Another period of tense silence ensued. Even the dullest boys in the class had perceived that something unusual was taking place. Beneath his gown, Mr Morris' joined hands twitched angrily.

'Well, bring it here, then, Fox. There's nothing so pathetic as a poor loser. Bring it here, boy, I say!' Mr Morris had actually raised his voice, some wholly unprecedented. Ferdy replied quietly.

'When I've finished it, sir.'

'Don't push it, Fox!'

'I'm sorry, sir, but we agreed that I would give you the book if I lost. Excuse me, but nothing was said about immediately.'

'Fox,' Morris almost growled.

'It's unheard of – to give someone a book you're in the middle of reading, isn't it?'

A breeze of agreement wafted from the class, careful not to show too openly its deep enjoyment of the scene. Morris, too, hid his feelings as best he could, intensely annoyed at being pushed out on a limb by this wet, Fox. He forced a smile.

'All right, Fox, a fair point. In victory, magnanimous – who said that, Napthine? You'll bring me the book at break tomorrow without fail.'

Melthorne turfed a junior boy out of the seat and sat down beside Ferdy, who was staring down out of the window watching the line of schoolboys climbing onto the bus, the conductor scowling at them like an armed guard.

'Blimey, Fox, you certainly made old Morris look a twat.'

Ferdy said nothing. Melthorne prattled on, only to stop when he realized his audience was not paying attention. He peered at Ferdy.

'You're crying, Fox.'

'I wish I hadn't found the bloody book.'

'Come on, don't worry about old Morris. He can't do anything – it's your property. He's wrong doing tricky deals like that, and he knows it.'

'I wish I hadn't found the bloody thing.'

Ferdy could not give the book up. He pretended to forget to go to the staff-room at break next day; in class, Mr Morris said he'd give him until Monday, but in a half-hearted sort of way. Ferdy simply gazed back without reacting and the history master shifted his eyes and shoved his fingers through his hair. The sight of what he took to be the headmaster's black gown hovering outside the translucent glass of the classroom door made Mr Morris let the matter drop for the present. He tossed back their history files. The class was fascinated now by Ferdy, but he ignored them. The only thing that counted was to get to the end of Professor Algol's little book, properly and without cheating.

III

It was the 'Last Great Correlator', as Algol termed it, that broke him. Three hundred words in, and the mental exhaustion arising from the effort of handling such a long chain forced him reluctantly to abandon the course. Unfortunately, the book was not willing to abandon him. At any moment his mind found itself unoccupied by the trivial concerns of everyday life, the words would recommence their tramp tramp tramp, goose-stepping past the review stand of his consciousness until the last word he could recall drew level whereupon the column of words all marked time tramp tramp tramp and he had to run upstairs to his room and feverishly look up the next word, and thereupon the words all about-turned and tramp tramp tramped past until the first word finally went by last. And then it would start again.

Four hundred words. Five hundred. Tack tack tack the metronome on his bedside table, tack tack tack almost constantly.

Now he had reached six hundred, the word 'Samson', and it was two o'clock in the morning. He switched off the light, not, as one might imagine, with relief, but with a spirit wearied at the prospect of yet further torment in its dreams, dreams now every bit as intense as waking life. It was the corridor again that he dreamt of, he was walking along it, cold dry and dark it was in there, while the metronome beat out every step he took. He knew that something was going to happen when he finally reached the end of the sequence, something irreversible. Back and forth he was permitted to travel the sequence, always it grew longer.

On the night when he finally reached the thousandth and ultimate word of the Last Great Correlator, everything stopped. The metronome died in mid-beat, he was no longer in his room, was at the end of the corridor, he hadn't know it had an end to it, and he was actually opening the door at the end of that long descending corridor. The door banged and clicked to behind him. Facing him stood a man, dressed in dusty black, and with a face of puffy, shiny white skin. Ferdy noticed nothing else, only this man in an empty featureless dark chamber, perhaps there was some sort of desk or block of something behind, somewhere in the shadows. The man spoke in a dry, creaky voice.

'Well, well, well. It's been rather a long time since I have had the pleasure of receiving a guest, but you are not altogether unexpected. Now, I imagine, if I do not flatter myself, you do not consider my claims to have been excessive. Memory and immortality. That was it, was it not? Well, Ferdy, we have such a long time together now. What happened? You still do not understand? Let us put it this way: your consciousness is now one with your memory, or, to be more accurate, with Memory. That's the secret, Ferdy. You have now achieved immortality within me, for memory can never die.'

'Off you go now,' said Algol, with a nod of almost paternal dismissal, and Ferdy found himself walking tramp tramp tramp up the dark corridor, past flickering paintings of long chains of captives kneeling in supplication, and when he reached the upper door, instead of fresh air and sunlight, it opened into a little room, a smell of formaldehyde, a bare dim light bulb, a little black book in his hand, and a creak on the stair.

Afterword

Born in 1950, I was educated at Dunstable Grammar School and graduated with an honours degree in English and American literature from the University of East Anglia. Thanks are very much due to my old masters at school, Mr William Frewin (English), Mr Alan Baxter (Latin) and Mr Brian Duncan (Geography); and to Prof. J B Broadbent, Prof. Russell Grice, Eric Homberger and Lorna Sage who put up with me at UEA and also to Malcolm Bradbury, Philip Larkin and Anthony Thwaite for their encouragement long ago.

Since leaving university I have been lucky enough to find work which has allowed me to live for extended periods abroad, including Italy, Germany, France, Greece, Spain, Egypt, Sri Lanka, the USA, Hong Kong, Ireland and Wales.

7322328R00097

Printed in Great Britain
by Amazon.co.uk, Ltd.,
Marston Gate.